D1234455

GOLF IS MADNESS

GOLF IS MADNESS

By TED BARNETT

Illustrations by Marcus Hamilton

A Golf Digest Book

Published by Golf Digest, Inc. **NYT**
A New York Times Company
495 Westport Avenue
Norwalk, Connecticut 06856

Trade book distribution by Simon and Schuster
A Division of Gulf & Western Corporation
New York, New York 10020
ISBN 0-671-22974-5

First printing
Library of Congress 77-80365
Manufactured in the United States of America

INTRODUCTION

Humor is an integral part of the game of golf—from first-tee negotiations to 19th hole postmortems—and fun and laughter somehow seem to flow naturally out of the anguish and disappointment as well as the thrills and excitement. Yet, for all its omnipresence on the course, golf humor is not easy to capture on paper. This is especially true of fiction and, aside from the late P. G. Wodehouse, it is difficult to recall a writer whose golf tales consistently evoke laughter. That's where Ted Barnett comes in.

Barnett is a Chicago advertising man who also has done such things as work on Mississippi riverboats and serve as president of a gold mine, all the while struggling through the decades with a golf handicap that has drifted steadily upward from 5 to 15.

"It's hard to accept that age may be the culprit," he says, "because actually I've never progressed beyond the age of eight. I like popsicles and the Three Stooges, I like to lie on the floor and play with the dog, I like the Marx Brothers. I like silly things, maybe because it's a subconscious effort not to take myself too seriously."

Barnett's wry, skeptical approach to life came to the attention of the editors of *Golf Digest* back in 1952, when the magazine was in its formative years, and they paid him the princely sum of $15 for a story entitled "Slamming Suki Sukiyuki." This proved to be one of the most popular things the magazine ever published and it has since been reprinted several times. Although clearly a marvelous spoof, the story attracted many letters from readers who wondered why Suki's feats could not be found in the record books.

Emboldened by the success of Suki, Barnett next sent *Golf Digest* the story of Pieter Van Schuyler, the gorilla who could drive a golf ball 400 yards. This classic entered the public domain so fast that Barnett never got proper credit for its invention. Another national magazine attributed it to Sam Snead a few weeks later and it wasn't long before Jack Paar gave the story ultimate exposure by repeating it before a vast television audience on the Tonight Show.

Barnett wrote a few more pieces for the magazine, then gradually drifted into real estate and away from the typewriter. A year or so back, however, he dusted off a few old manuscripts he found in his attic, sat down and wrote a few new ones and shipped everything to Bill Davis, president of Golf Digest, who had been Barnett's original contact 25 years earlier. Davis, who knows full well that good golf humor is as scarce as a double eagle, remembered Suki and Pieter and other moments of laughter and agreed that it should all be gathered together for a new generation of golf readers.

The collection on the following pages is the unforeseen result of the author's decision, made many years ago, to enter journalism school "because I thought I'd look good in a trench coat working between London and Paris."

But instead of London and Paris, he can be found in Winnetka, Illinois—in doubleknits—working on a golf swing that may be deteriorating, but is still pretty good for an 8-year-old.

—*The Editors*

CONTENTS

The Sporting People 9

Slamming Suki Sukiyuki 21

The Marmaduke Massacre 27

The Foursome 35

The Lowest Round on Record 51

Best Terrier, Fastest Girl 55

Golf Is a Game of Madness 65

The Golf God 71

The Story of Pieter Van Schuyler 83

The Golfer 87

THE SPORTING PEOPLE

When Harry Bassler won his fifth Open and his sixth Masters nobody was much surprised. And when he finally put it all together with another British Open title and another PGA the only real surprise was that Harry hadn't won The Grand Slam earlier. After all, he hit the ball longer and straighter than anybody else, his irons were superior and his putting was a lot better than any other golfer on the tour. Harry Bassler's only rough edge was his sand play. But then Harry didn't visit much sand. The big redhead dominated golf so completely, there was talk that his appearance in a tournament cut the gate and knocked down the TV ratings. Something had to be done to take the ho-hum out of golf, and Harry did it. He disappeared.

Harry's disappearance launched the biggest manhunt since Judge Crater. He re-surfaced three weeks later near Cape Kennedy, Fla. He was found in a dazed condition and was immediately hospitalized for observation. The diagnosis: nervous breakdown.

The following is Bassler's own story of his three-week disappearance. It has been cleared and discounted by the FBI:

"After the Crosby tournament, I decided to skip the Napa Valley thing and go down to L.A. for a couple of business meetings. Benny Zatz, my manager, had an idea for an instructional TV series one of the networks was hot for. We also had a meeting set up on a real estate deal, and I wanted to buy a sailboat.

"I checked into a bungalow at the Canyon Hills Hotel, and I was walking through the garden toward the Coyote Lounge when it happened. My legs felt rubbery and I began to fall, but I fell *up*. It was that sickening, falling feeling, only reversed, as if gravity had failed. I was so scared I couldn't yell, and there was nobody around to hear me anyway. At 6:00 in L.A., everyone's either in a car or a bar. I remember two things about the hotel. As I tumbled up past the third floor, there was a little kid and an English bulldog looking out a window. Their heads both slowly inclined upward as they watched me heading for the sky. Then, after I'd soared several hundred feet above the hotel, I noticed that across the entire roof, from one side to the other, were the words: 'Hotel Bon Air.' They were cracked, faded and worn, but unmistakable.

"I went higher and higher. I saw the Civic Center and the ocean and several jets in glide patterns heading toward L.A. International. I saw Hollywood Park Race Track across from the airport, and the Channel Islands.

"I knew I was dead. There couldn't be any other explanation. I must have had a heart attack and was now on my way to heaven. But the soul went to heaven, I reasoned, not the body. I pinched my knee; definite feeling there. I began hurtling faster and faster. Up, up through a heavy cloud layer and still faster. It became very cold. I had often wondered if people in non-instantaneous fatal accidents like airplane crashes, or in cars that went sailing over cliffs, had time to think about what was happening to them. I know the answer now. It's no. As you achieve maximum velocity, you open your eyes and mouth as wide as possible and you scream from your toes. Finally, in the midst of all that cold, tumbling terror I blacked out.

"The next thing I remember, I was standing on the first tee of the most incredible golf course I had ever seen. The setting was mountainous and tropical, like Tahiti, Hawaii or somewhere in the Grenadines. I could see inlets and coves and great stretches of blue-green water.

"Lush fairways lined with tall royal palms split through giant, jagged rock outcroppings. Hibiscus, bougainvillea and orchids bloomed everywhere. The sky was a faint, turquoise blue, the air cool and windless.

"To the right of the tee stood a group of 20 or 25 people, male and female, dressed in silk, brocade and velvet-looking robes and gowns. They were masked, and the masks were ornate and generally humorous. They included looks of pop-eyed amazement, impudence or coquettishness. There was a Laurel mask, and a Hardy mask, and even a Richard Nixon mask. These people were quite

10

animated; they talked noisily and laughed among themselves. They had the look of a medieval royal court, and their language was something I had never heard in all of my travels. It was more musical than spoken.

"A man wearing a cross-eyed bird mask approached and handed me a scroll written in English by some kind of electronic equipment. It said that my skills were known and that I was being given the opportunity to play (match play) for ' The Championship. ' Following this brief message a hole-by-hole breakdown of the course was displayed in minute detail. Overlaid on aerial photographs were yardage figures from dozens of points plus notes on traps, trees, rocks and water. To my astonishment the course was more than 12,000 yards long, with several par-5's at about an even thousand.

"An eruption of noise from the group made me look up. They all had noisemakers going: rattles, whirligigs, gongs, sirens, bells and whistles. Then they began to point excitedly. I turned. Stepping onto the tee was the biggest, toughest-looking man I had ever seen.

"He was the eternal jock, but a lot bigger—close to nine feet tall. He had a bullet head with a crew cut, no neck, and sloped shoulders. His eyes were deep set, and he had high cheek bones, thick lips and a massive chin. He was stripped to the waist and wore what looked like a Roman legionnaire's skirt. He bowed first to the group and then to me. I bowed back.

"I wondered why I felt so good after all that fright and freezing cold. I was actually pumped-up to play. But how could I play without my sticks? With that, the noisemaking seemed to intensify and there was more pointing. Two little girls, slightly built and stark naked, came to the tee carrying golf bags. They couldn't have been more than 10 or 11 years old and their heads were shaved. They were apparently very strong, because they toted the bags without effort.

"This nakedness, as contrasted to the overdressed gallery, pointed up some kind of caste situation. The girls were naked, my opponent was half-naked, and the gallery

11

members were in varying degrees of dress and over-dress.

"One of the little girls bowed and set the bag down next to me. No question about it: the bag was mine. I don't know how they got it there, but they did. I was also supplied with plenty of balls and tees, several gloves, and even a pair of golf shoes. The man with the bird mask pointed back and forth between me and the big guy—it was some kind of an eenie, meenie, minee, mo—and the big guy got the honor. We were ready to go.

"The first fairway sloped downward at about a 30-degree angle for 127 yards, according to my map, where it then ended at a chasm filled with roiling waters. Far across the chasm the fairway resumed, slanting upward and then doglegging out of sight. My opponent selected a driver with a shaft that had to be seven feet long. Swinging one-handed with a giant and graceful arc, he crashed by far the longest drive I had ever seen. It soared far over the chasm and up the slope where it finally died in the knee of the dogleg.

"The map said it was 127 to the chasm, 214 across, and 125 to the dogleg. That made his drive 466 yards. Hell, I couldn't even drive the chasm! I took out a wedge and hit a little poop shot down the fairway. The gallery erupted with their noisemakers at my display of cowardice. Next, I hit a good 2-wood over the water, but I was still nowhere near the big guy's drive.

"The whole entourage traipsed over the bridge and up the fairway to my ball. I went on up to the corner to see what the possibilities were. It was time to gamble. The hole was guarded by the big palms. If I could hit a 5-wood high enough and draw it, I could maybe get home, some 255 yards away. I caught it good but not quite high enough. The ball hit square in the crown of the tree and dropped straight down.

"It was my opponent's turn and he calmly flicked a 200-yard 7-iron, stone dead. I picked up. One down. Hole No. 2 was an island par-3 of 317 yards. The island was circular, about a quarter of a mile in diameter; it was located out in a cove, with access by motor launch. The green was centered, but the rest of the island was all sand trap. I can drive 317 yards but at a very low angle. I figured any shot that reached would richochet off the green like a bullet off a tin roof. My only chance was to hit it into the trap and then blast close.

"The big guy hit a four-iron so high I couldn't believe it would reach. It hit in front of the hole, took one soft hop, rimmed the cup and ended up about a foot away. I hit a super shot into the trap, and blasted out two feet short. Two down.

"I lost holes three, four, and five to incredible birdies, including some drives that made the legendary long hitters look like school children. Thomson, Bayer, Dent and a few others may have hit long drives in their day, but this big dude with his one-handed slap was going out nearly twice as long as those boys, and with deadly accuracy. He hit it where he wanted it, and with the proper draw or fade.

"I didn't know why this match was set up, or where I was, or who the strange, robed people were, but I was not accustomed to losing. This was *my* game, and nobody takes five holes in a row off me and gets away with it. But I couldn't outgun the guy, and I couldn't even touch him for touch. So I had to try something else. Match play means Walter Hagen, and Walter Hagen means psychology. I never thought I'd have to use this weapon, but I was beginning to run out of holes.

"The big question was whether or not my big friend would be receptive. We had a language barrier, for starters, and he was about as animated as a stuffed buffalo. He never cracked an expression through the first five holes, and he only looked at me twice. Both times it was right through me, like I was a fire hydrant.

"At this point I had to get through to shake things up or I was finished. I started the campaign on No. 6. Banking on the idea that the amount of clothing worn had some connection with caste in this place, and the fact that my opponent was stripped to the waist, I unzipped my bag and pulled out an old yellow rain slicker. I put it on and pulled the hood over my head. The gallery recognized this bit of

13

gamesmanship and whooped it up with the noisemakers. The big guy looked at me, teed up and hit out of bounds into the ocean. The noisemakers clattered. He teed up again and poled one straight down the pike just short of the green 475 yards away. I drove straight and hit a 4-iron onto the green. He burned the cup with his chip. I got down in two for a winner, and another eruption of noise came from the gallery.

"The 7th hole had the chasm again. The chart said 310 would carry. A light wind had come up and was in back of me, so I knew I could make it. I invoked Sir Walter again. I took my driver, lined up the shot, stopped and consulted the chart, went through some fake mental anguish, then shook my head and exchanged the driver for an 8-iron, as if I had decided to lay up. I glanced at the big fellow and saw a faint smile. I lined up the shot, started the swing, then stopped and exchanged back for the driver. I then conked one right on the nose over the chasm. The noisemakers went bananas.

"The big guy looked like he was in pain. He pulled his drive way left and into a grove of what looked like eucalyptus trees. He hit a tree on his next shot, while I hit a perfect 3-iron to the green. His recovery was short and he chipped close. I knocked my putt in for the hole. More noisemakers.

"As we walked to the 8th tee I noticed the sun was still in our face. I turned around. It was at our back, too. Yes, and to our right. Three suns. Discovering the suns settled one question in my mind: these people were not oil-rich Arabs on some private playground in the Aegean Sea. This was indeed another world, in another kind of solar system, though remarkably similar to our own.

"Another thing that finally penetrated was the incredible surveillance system these people must have. I have no notion of the spatial distance involved, but golf on earth had been monitored to the smallest details. The equipment, the tees, the greens, the pins—all were identical to ours. I also realize that the outstanding features of many of the premier courses in the United States had been incorporated into this magnificent layout.

"For example, my second shot on No. 7 was the home shot on the 18th at Doral. The approach on No. 6 was the entire 8th hole at Pebble Beach. I looked through the charts and found parts of Winged Foot, Mauna Kea, Butler National, Pine Valley, Medinah No. 3, Oakmont, Augusta National and others. Mix in cliffs, chasms, islands, palm trees and an extra 5,000 yards, the result was the ultimate golf course. As a designer and builder of courses, I recognized this one as perfect in every detail of engineering, layout and conditioning. Totally magnificent.

"We were playing No. 8 now and the big guy had a five-footer for a half. As he lined it up I remembered another Hagen ploy. I held up my hand to interrupt him, then picked up his ball and tossed it to him, thus conceding the hole.

"A few moments later, on No. 9, he had only about a four-footer to halve the hole. He looked at me expectantly. I folded my arms, turned and looked out to sea. His putt was an inch short. I was only two down after 9 holes, and I had this guy going.

"One of the worst features of tournament golf in the United States is the tasteless hot dog and the warm beer served out of striped tents. This feature had also been duplicated, and for lunch I tentatively nibbled on a dog. It tasted dreadfully authentic. The big fellow inhaled 13 of them with onions and mustard, plus three replica Baby Ruth bars.

"I lost 10 with a bird to his eagle. Three down.

"On 11 I went Hagen again. It was a 500-yard par-4 with a dogleg right. According to the chart the short way was possible, so I hatched a plan. As expected, the big fellow's drive was a 400-yarder that he faded expertly around the corner. I selected the 4-wood, a club I never use, and hit a shot that started out down the center and then sliced violently into an apparent jail. I let out a string of choice words at the top of my lungs and then methodically bashed my 4-wood to pieces on a large rock.

"The gallery was stunned except for the guy in the

Laurel mask who clacked his whirligig at me, either in admonition for my poor sportsmanship or in appreciation of my ploy. When we got down to my ball I went through more fake anguish, then took out a 7-iron as if to chip back into the fairway. In the middle of the backswing I stopped, put the club back in the bag, selected a 3-iron and absolutely creamed a shot over the trees and home.

"The gallery erupted with babbling and noisemakers. The big guy spread his arms in disbelief and appeal. Several in the gallery mocked the pose and the sirens and whistles shrilled derisively. He turned back to the ball and skulled it over the green and deep into the woods. I was back to only 2 down.

"We halved 12, 13, 14 and 15 with birdies, the big guy consistently knocking the ball so stiff he nearly holed it twice. My shortest approach on these par-4's was 255 yards, so my birds were three chip-ins and an 80-foot putt. Still 2 down.

"On 16 the big fellow needed a three-and-a-half-footer for a half to become dormie. He implored me with his eyes to concede it. I looked at the sky. He yipped it a foot wide. One down.

"On 17 he had a four-footer on a crown, a putt I wouldn't want. I had him yipping, but I was afraid he might luck it in. Like all good yippers though, he froze over the ball and was locked in total paralysis for two full minutes. Finally the backswing came, slow and palsied, and then a stab. The putt was dead true, just a hair strong. It hit the back of the cup, jumped half an inch, and stayed on the edge. Match even.

"We walked to the 18th tee through a concrete tunnel, our footsteps echoing off the walls. It reminded me of the tunnels through the hills at the Bel Air Country Club in California. We stepped into a silent lift and after a few moments emerged at the highest point on the golf course.

"What a fantastic setting for a home hole. Directly in back of us rose sheer, black cliffs several thousand feet high. They stretched left and right for five or six miles, defining the lush peninsula below. From the top of the cliff to the right poured a waterfall with the bulk of the American Falls at Niagara, but easily 20 times the height. This roaring mass of water raced through the chasm that crisscrossed the course and came into play on almost every hole.

"From this height I could see, far to the left where the cliffs met the sea, a series of interlocking geometric shapes. It was unmistakably a tennis complex, with dozens upon dozens of courts arrayed in star-shaped clusters, probably for instructional purposes. I had no doubt that there was a track and field complex somewhere nearby, a swimming complex and sophisticated facilities for team sports. If golf was a good example, these people were into sports at a level yet unattained on earth.

"The 18th hole was 1,118 yards, a par-5. The roaring torrent from the falls ran down the right side of the hole, then bent back cutting across the center and down the left side, then left across the center again, and then once again in front of the green. In effect, the hole consisted of three buttes separated by the crisscrossing gorge.

"I consulted the chart. The first chasm was out 285. To carry it would require 330. The alternative was to lay up. But if I did that I would need close to 400 to clear the next chasm. No way. If I did any laying up at all, the best I could do was get on in 4. I would almost concede the big guy getting on in 3, and if he did I was beaten. I had to go for it.

"I teed high, took an extra-long backswing and hit the ball a ton harder than I'd hit one since my sophomore year in high school. I fell down on my knees from the momentum. Nailed it perfect. Then the big guy stepped up and knocked one 100 yards farther with that big, lazy swing of his.

"Looking at the chart, I saw that my second shot was essentially like the first—about a 300-yard carry to clear the second chasm. I needed a super lie because I wanted to hit the driver again. It sat up high, like a puffball, and I creamed it right to left, over the narrowest width. My opponent hit what was, for him, a skyball. It came down not six feet from my ball.

"More and more robed and masked figures were moving in from all directions, and the sounds of the noisemakers became strident and steady. Until now, the big guy had probably put away all of his opponents long before this. The word had no doubt gone out that today he had a slight problem. By the time we got up to where the balls lay, white robes lined the fairway all the way to the green, and the noise swelled clamorously.

"My second shot lay closest to the hole, so I bowed to my opponent. The big guy promptly hit a 5-iron a mile high in the air and dead on the stick all the way. It missed the pin by a whisper, landed two feet beyond, and then jumped back to within six inches. I had to hole out from 341 yards to win, or knock it stiff for a half. There was again no question of laying up. If I did that, I'd have to chip in from maybe 100 yards. The lie was good again, so I took out the driver for the third time on the hole. I jumped all over it and caught it flush, right in the screws. We were slightly above the green, so I could see the whole action. The ball had to clear the chasm (a distance of 288 yards). It landed scarcely two feet on the other side, took a big hop between the traps and hit the pin dead center with a big "Whang"! The ball jumped six feet in the air and then drove straight down into the hole.

"The big guy saw it all. He uttered a hoarse scream and started running. I could hear the sounds of the noisemakers begin to rise—the gongs, whistles, rattles, bells, clackers and whirligigs. The big guy was running back up the fairway, but a dozen robed figures still working their noisemakers moved in from the sides and cut him off. He turned and ran down the slope toward the sea, but several other groups of masked and robed figures had anticipated his route and were moving methodically to intercept him. Then I saw something distant but unmistakable that was as funny as it was horrible. Down on the beach, at the end of the growing gauntlet of people, a man wearing a black hood stood leaning on a large, bladed axe, patiently, as if he'd been through this many times. Next to him was a chopping block with a neck notch. Ever since I was a kid I'd seen this guy in comic books and Boris Karloff horror movies. He was a ridiculous B-thriller, Saturday afternoon cliché, and yet I felt the same wave of fear now as I had felt then.

"The big guy veered hysterically to the right only to be confronted with a dozen or so robed figures. Then he ran to the left, but still another group appeared, blocking his flight. He made several hysterical attacks, tossing robed figures around like rag dolls, but more and more appeared.

"Inevitably, his zig-zag course brought him closer and closer to the executioner. Behind the black figure, a host of white-gowned people began to assemble in anticipation. Naked young girls with shaved heads, their arms full of what looked like shooting sticks, stood by. The robed figures now took the sticks from them and sat down.

"I had to do something. Obviously, losing was intolerable to these people. But what a magnificent match the giant had played. On a 12,000-yard course he had carded about a 62 in a display of power and touch unparalleled in my experience. My card was at least a half-dozen strokes higher, but I had lucked out with a combination of psychology and flukes, culminated by a Lew Worsham at 18. That a man should die after that kind of effort was unthinkable.

"I charged down the hill waving my driver like a saber. But the robed figures, who were moving quietly now from all directions toward the forming tableau, paid no attention to me. I galloped through their ranks and down across the brilliantly green, palm-lined fairways. The crowd parted to let me through.

"It grew quiet; the noisemakers stopped. The man with the funny bird mask stepped forward and handed me a scroll. It read simply: 'You are the Champion.' Then the big fellow bowed ceremoniously followed by the executioner, the little girls, the sporting people, all bowing formally from the waist. Now the noisemakers came out, and the banging and whistling rose again until it filled the mind. I stepped forward to protest the fate of my opponent when suddenly I was flung high into the air, my arms and legs thrashing wildly. I accelerated sickeningly and screamed in terror.

"I entered a sea of mist that grew darker as I raced upward. I closed my eyes, curled into a cannonball, and listened to my hurtling body create a strange *shhhh* sound. My mind went blank. The next thing I knew I was standing in front of a Texaco station in Cape Kennedy, Fla."

Epilogue: The Sporting People, it seems, were as generous with the victors as they were harsh with the vanquished. And they were as diffident as they were rich. The awarding of a cup, a trophy, or a large sum of money would have been to them a tasteless and repugnant act. Subtle measures must always be employed.

Harry Bassler flew to the West Coast from Cape Kennedy and found that his golf clubs, minus the 4-wood, were in the trunk of his car at the Coyote Hills Hotel. Unfortunately, Harry never did discover the precious gems that had been placed in the cores of the golf balls he carried in his golf bag. The stones were diamonds, rubies, emeralds, and sapphires averaging 15 to 20 carats in weight, flawless and beautifully cut. There were 37 stones in all, but most of them are still inside a dozen rotting Titleists that lie embedded in the mud of several nameless golf course creeks and ponds. However, it is believed that two emeralds and a diamond, with a total value of about $450,000 are still bouncing around inside three tough, new red-ringed covers at a driving range in New Jersey.

SLAMMING
SUKI SUKIYUKI

There was a Japanese golf professional of the swank Hamilton Country Club in Bombay, India, who caused more of a furor in international golfing circles, until his untimely death in 1924, than any Bobby Jones or Walter Hagen.

Suki Sukiyuki Jr., known to his fans as "Slamming Suki," was probably the only golfer in history to win a major golf championship right-handed one year, and left-handed the next. He accomplished this remarkable feat in capturing the British Open in 1919 and 1920.

The bright star of Suki's fame faded, however, when his unparalleled triumphs were disallowed by the sacrosanct Royal and Ancient Golf Club on the grounds that he had employed to his own advantage a type of follow-through not sanctioned in British play. This follow-through, not uncommon among Asiatic golfers, consisted of striking the ball twice in a single swing stroke. Slow motion movies brought the fact to light, however, and thus Suki's record-smashing 275 in 1920, his left-handed year, was actually 550.

Born the son of well-to-do peasants in the Honshu province of Japan, Suki spent his early childhood in the Honshu tradition—breeding goldfish and skiing on the slopes of Mt. Fujiyama. Suki Sr., however, soon realized that his young son was in need of schooling of a more formal nature than was then available locally, and sent him post-haste to a private school in Tokyo. One day a group of boys from the school went out to the Imperial Links to see a golfing exhibition by the famous Duncan MacPhee, who was then on a world-wide barnstorming tour. From that day forward Suki was a slave to the game. His wealthy parents had him outfitted and arranged to have him take instruction from Tama Shanti, the Japanese champion. This was unfortunate in that Shanti was an exponent of the aforementioned illegal follow-through. Suki, for

21

his part, was an apt pupil and within nine months had officially taken Shanti to the cleaners, becoming the new champion of all Japan, a title he never relinquished.

Seeking new fields to conquer, Suki entered the Chinese Closed at Hong Kong in 1910. It was there that he inadvertently discovered his amazing ambidexterity. On the 18th hole of the final round, needing but a triple bogey to win, Suki was in trouble. He had hooked his drive into a rice paddy, blasted out and into a small forest of yew trees and, on his third shot, rolled up tight against the right side of a small ornamental pagoda. His cushion was fast deflating. The hot Chinese sun was pouring down. Suki took off his pith helmet and mopped his sloping brow. What to do?

He assayed the impossible lie, his grinning opponent and the green some 290 yards away. Smiling thoughtfully, he drew from his bag an adjustable club which some admirer had given him after the Japanese Open the year before. He had never used it, but had carried it in his bag as a kind of good luck piece. Now was certainly the time for it! Setting it for a left-handed driving iron position, he wound up and struck. The shot was one of those low screamers, straight as a chopstick, that began to rise slowly and then almost ascended to the heavens. The direction was true, the distance was perfect, and Suki had holed out, left-handed, from almost 300 yards away. This became the famous "Pagoda Shot" and heralded a new era for "Slamming Suki" Sukiyuki.

After Hong Kong, Suki dropped out of competition for six weeks, bought himself a set of left-handed clubs and practiced intently. He found that left-handed he was just as proficient as right-handed, if not more so. He decided to enter the Shanghai Open and play strictly left-handed. He won, going away, by 16 strokes.

For the next two years Suki dominated the Far Eastern scene. He swept through the Opens at Peiping and Peping, won the Specialists at Vladivostok and the World Wide at Bangkok. He played sometimes right-handed, sometimes left-handed, sometimes a combination of the two. His unique skill came in particularly handy when he was up against a tree.

After garnering every conceivable Far Eastern trophy, Slamming Suki made plans to sail for England, where competition was stiffer. This project was, however, postponed by World War I. Suki volunteered for the Imperial Navy but he was rejected for triple-jointedness. Heartbroken, he returned to his home in the Honshu province. There he remained, out of the public eye, for several months. Then, returning to Tokyo, he joined the J.S.O., Japanese equivalent of the U.S.O., and spent the war years entertaining the troops with his amazingly ambidextrous tap dancing. He would dance sometimes on his right foot, and sometimes on his left.

With the close of the War, Slamming Suki made good his plan for a tour of the British Isles. He arrived early in 1919, just in time for the Ulster Open. Suki immediately became the darling of the galleries. He was physically unprepossessing, but his toothy grin, owl eyes behind thick, black horn-rimmed glasses, and, of course, his booming shots from either side captivated the golfing public. This tournament saw him nosed out by his old idol, MacPhee, but, since it was Suki's first golf competition in over four years he was not discouraged.

The year of 1919 was one that will not soon be forgotten by those who know golf. It was, of course, the year of Suki's "Big Sweep" of British Golf. He won the British Open right-handed, the Irish Sweepstakes left-handed, the Scotch Lowball right-handed and, to cap everything, the Welsh PGA Championship alternating left- and right-handed strokes.

Suki's fame was unparalleled. He was feted in all of the golfing capitals of the British Isles. The King himself paid him a visit in the lawnmower shed of the famous Royal Potrush course. Suki was using this as a locker room, following his win in the British Open, since at that time professionals were still denied the use of clubhouse facilities at British courses.

Soon after the 1920 Open, however, the shocking truth

of his "double hit" technique, which had led to Slamming Suki's amazing successes, was bared to the world via the slow motion camera. After returning his many laurels to assorted second-place winners, Suki packed his bag, took his two sets of clubs and set sail for Bombay, India, and the Hamilton Country Club. He vowed never again to set foot in the Western World.

Suki remained at Hamilton, as professional in residence, until one sad day in 1924. He was in the Bombay station waiting for a train to Karachi, where he was to defend his Indian Invitational title. Becoming impatient, he stepped onto the track to see if the train was coming. He was instantly struck by the incoming express and hurled to the next track where he was struck on the right side by an outgoing local. Thus Slamming Suki Sukiyuki died as he had lived—ambidextrously.

THE MARMADUKE MASSACRE

Enormous black cumulus clouds came crawling in over the Atlantic. Raindrops the size of half dollars splattered the already squishy fairways and greens of The Marmaduke Cricket Club. The galleries huddled under ponchos, slickers, soggy hats and umbrellas that looked like giant flowers. It was a foul northeaster, but the lightning that stabbed the course intermittently was the big problem, and play had stopped for the fifth time in three days.

The galleries suffered in all the water and mud, but the pros felt no discomfort. Harvey Fistula had some ham and eggs. Stash O'Neill relaxed in a sauna. Ronny Grits took a nap. Cap Cruller played bridge. And it was rumored that Al Macaroon went for a swim.

All the pros, in fact, were snugly ensconced in their own private, motorized clubhouses on wheels, havens of incredible luxury that carried them around the golf courses hole by hole, shot by shot. The age of the supervan had arrived. And long before the tournament at Marmaduke ended, these same supervans, along with the frustrations they caused and the dreadful weather conditions, combined to trigger the darkest, most disgraceful day in the history of professional golf.

The supervan was a bad idea that got carried away. At their final evolution many of the vans were incredibly sophisticated, air-conditioned land yachts the size of Greyhound buses and cost as much as $1 million.

The crews usually included a driver, caddie (who no longer carried clubs, but had become an officious go-fer), meteorologist, business manager, agent, nurse, masseur, maid, cook and coach (often a retired pro). The master suite in the supervans often accommodated wives and children, parents or girl friends. At any given time there could be as many as a dozen people aboard.

Standard equipment in the supervans included CB radio-telephones; television to monitor the tournament coverage (including the leader-board) plus a closed-circuit system to replay shots for swing analysis; complete weather system (including radar, barograph, thermograph, anemograph and anemometer); rangefinder for plotting distances to the fraction of an inch; small shop for club repair; kitchen, lounge, guest bedroom, and the aforementioned master suite. The supervans were fully equipped command posts in which the stratagems for the battles were devised and honed. Some super customized models included such niceties as saunas, whirlpool baths, pool tables, bars and the rumored Macaroon swimming pool.

The supervans had elaborate custom exteriors reflecting the personalities and business obligations of the owners. The Harvey Fistula van was fire-engine red with large portraits of a smiling Harvey wearing a sombrero. Replicas and logotypes of the products he endorsed graced the sides. The Al Macaroon van was pale blue and, in addition to the constantly whirling radar antenna on top, it had a small glassed-in observation dome. The Grits, Winkleton and Fujikawa vans were done in their school colors. Pizzicato and Jarvis went for psychedelics. Others were done in stripes, polka dots, rainbows, murals, sunbursts and even a camouflage design. To accommodate these six- and seven-ton monsters, highway engineers had to design roadways paralleling each hole on every tournament course in the world. Every bridge over every creek and pond had to be scrapped and rebuilt at a staggering cost.

All the pros had vans. Some were simple Volkswagen or Econolines, also used by the rabbits and rookies to get from town to town. Some vans were provided by the clubs and had temporary name cards glued on the sides. These cheap and sterile peasant vans may have lacked the material advantages, but in a showdown against a million-dollar land-cruiser they had the whole gallery cheering them on. Americans love the underdog.

The golf vans were a natural evolution in American golf. First, the golfer was on his own, alone to make the decision on a shot or putt. Next, the caddie emerged from the shadows of ignorance and servitude as a full-blown expert on all phases of the game. It got so bad that a professional golfer would not dream of hitting the ball without the counsel and approval of his caddie, who would often shake his head in disapproval and firmly point out the proper course of action. The era of the coach changed all this and opened up great new job opportunities for over-the-hill pros.

The pros loved supervan life, and their scores improved steadily until soon every course record and every tournament record had been broken. It was a shame that the player had to actually hit the ball, because this was the only area that defied science. In spite of pin-point preparation, the pro would occasionally push, duck-hook, scuff or top a shot, causing a chorus of angry babble from the supervan. Yet scores continued to crawl downward until a victory in the baked-out Southwest required four rounds in the high 50's.

On the negative side, all the pros got fat from lack of exercise and from the availability of bowls of chili and banana cream pie between shots. Not just round, like Bob Murphy or Billy Casper, but fat like a bunch of young Sidney Greenstreets. They became jiggling, waddling fat people with jowels, triple-chins and tummies that bulged over their $50 alligator belts.

But the big effect of the supervans was on the attitude of the galleries. They hated and despised the whole idea. Not only had the slim, bronzed gods they loved and lionized turned into pudgy hedonists, they were seldom seen. After an intolerable analysis period in the supervan command post, the pro would step out, hit, and pop back inside. And when the "tent rule" was approved by the rules committees, the players were seen even less. Before this rule was passed, players were not allowed to have an umbrella held over them during a downpour or any other time, because it could interfere with the shot. After the passage of the tent rule, large and gaudy tents 20 feet square and open on the hole side were set up around the ball whenever the pro so chose. Thus the only time most of the gallery saw him was while he was leaving the van to enter the tent, and vice versa.

Fan reaction to the fatness, the supervans and the tents first erupted during the second round of the U.S. Open. Leading money-winner Bobo Pastiche was lining up a putt in the usual hushed silence when a voice yelled, "Blow it, fatty!" Pastiche looked up, glared, then hunched over the ball again. From the opposite side of the green a lady yelled, "Look out, Tubby!" Again Pastiche straightened up. He gestured for the marshals.

"Have those people removed from the course," he ordered.

The gallery reacted with hoots, yells, catcalls and laughter, as the frustrations of the supervan years finally boiled over, followed by a unison chant which was to become standard around the greens.

"Yip! Yip! Yip! Yip! Yip! Yip! Yip! Yip!"

Pastiche retreated into his supervan. And as van after van got stacked up behind him, frantic walkie-talkie action produced the entire tournament committee, who first attempted to reason with the crowd and, failing this, ordered Pastiche to continue play.

The press and the broadcast media considered this heckling breakthrough as a positive development. It was reasoned that a quarterback or a baseball pitcher had an immensely more sophisticated chore to perform than a golfer. Yet the golfer was somehow granted the right to complete silence and lack of even the slightest visual distraction, while the quarterback and the pitcher were screamed at by 50,000 or more people.

Although heckling was at first confined to the greens, it soon spread to the tees and throughout the course. It gave professional golf a whole new atmosphere. In the past whenever a great yell erupted, it had signified a canned snake or a lipped blast. Now the entire course was alive with yelling as the public gave it to their plump, rich ex-darlings. Then came the tomato and egg era.

It started at the Mohair Open with a cream pie. Harvey

Fistula was addressing the ball on the first tee when a society lady pied him in the face. Fistula's picture, looking like something out of Laurel and Hardy, made all the papers. The lady was jailed for assault. The public loved the pie idea, but not the penalty. The anonymity of the ripe tomato or rotten egg heaved out of a crowd provided total protection, and by the second round the fans were filling the air with them.

The pros immediately struck and refused to play. The sponsors, tired of the inflated demands of the pudgy pros, said, "No tickee, no washee." And so the play and the barrage continued.

The heckling, the tomatoes and the eggs caused profound changes in professional golf. Attendance boomed. The new era attracted masses of people who had no interest whatsoever in golf. They came to molest. They were the same kind of people who had packed the colosseums in Roman times. The sponsors were forced to hire many more security people and set up an airport-type shakedown system designed to filter out the foul-smelling missiles. In fact, however, the sponsors seized the opportunity to double the entrance fees and instructed the guards to look the other way. Why kill the golden goose?

The pros themselves beefed up their supervan staffs with their own security police, with one riding "shot-gun" on top. The rain tents became a necessity for all shots, even putts, and were constructed of wood, hinged for easy set-up and take-down.

As conditions deteriorated, so did the golf scores. The heaviness of the players and their constant apprehension about being struck by flying objects hoisted even the winning scores into the 80's. Relations between the players and the galleries grew steadily worse, and shakedowns for contraband missiles and fist fights became commonplace. The situation escalated when opportunists invented egg and tomato launchers that combined distance and accuracy.

But bad as things were, the money was good, and so a nervous status quo was maintained. Only three or four of the older pros took the opportunity to retire, so the tour went on.

The Marmaduke Cricket Club was tailor-made for a riot. As a bastion of prejudice and privilege, it had no peer on the eastern seaboard. The club was so exclusive, it was often said that even the members couldn't get in. Add that to the supervans, chubby pros, heckling fans, rotten eggs, and overripe tomatoes, plus a near hurricane, and you had fireworks looking for a match.

The spark was provided by a Puerto Rican lady named Bella Cortez, who tried to enter the clubhouse bathroom and was denied. So her six brothers bashed the clubhouse door down, and with that the "Marmaduke Massacre" was on.

Inside of 15 minutes, the clubhouse was stripped of every item of value, including trophies, portraits, silverware and rare China. The walls and the ceilings were plastered with foul missiles; the furniture and windows were all smashed. Out on the course, tee markers and flags were destroyed or stolen. Several vans were surrounded, rocked and tipped over. Four supervans collided at high speed while converging on the only escape route. Soon the remaining vans had gathered together in the center of the Marmaduke Polo Field and formed a tight circle like so many covered wagons of the wild west. Within this ring, the pros and their 500-odd crew members, armed with golf clubs, were battling the vast crowd when the entire personnel of a nearby U.S. Navy base responded to their calls for help.

The Marmaduke Massacre miraculously counted no deaths or serious injuries. It did, however, cause sweeping reform. On the following day the commissioner handed down the harshest dictum since the Kenesaw Mountain Landis decisions at the time of the 1919 Black Sox scandal.

The golf commissioner decreed:
1. No galleries for the foreseeable future. The pros will play for TV revenues only.
2. No supervans or any form of transportation.

3. No advice or assistance, including putting tips.
4. Get rid of the fat, or else. Each pro will be given a weight-loss schedule and will weigh in before each tournament. Noncompliance will result in suspension.
5. If and when galleries are re-admitted, there will be no heckling or distractions allowed. Gallery members will be ejected for noncompliance.

Within six months the pros were thin again and galleries were re-admitted to the tournaments.

The supervans are still rolling in countries like Yemen, Qatar and Kuwait, and such middle eastern cities as Al-Basrah, Abu Dhabi and Dubai. The air-conditioned luxury of these cruisers was made for the oil countries. The Arabs snapped them up for money, and they can be seen today enroute to O.P.E.C. meetings in capitol cities, or to fun and games at secluded oases. And on the sides of the supervans, fading steadily in the desert sun and sand, you can still discern names like "Bobo Pastiche" and "Al Macaroon," with here and there a minute particle of rotten egg or ripe tomato.

THE FOURSOME

Until the golfers arrive, Harry's Hamburgatorium at the top of the Bronx almost snores its way into Sunday morning. Harry's is a cop stop and draws a few hustlers and bus drivers. But when the late show crowd from The Granada Movie Palace around the corner goes home, the only action at Harry's is Koko, the Puerto Rican cook, dancing to the top 40. Then around 3:00 a.m., the joint goes up for grabs.

It starts with a very faint rendition of "The Bridge on the River Kwai" theme played on a set of distant automobile air horns.

"Here they come!" says Koko. The theme plays again, louder and from a different direction. Then again from still another direction, and another. The themes begin to lay on and overlap each other. And louder and louder. It's like Harry's is a four-alarm fire with Colonel Bogey instead of sirens.

Then the first big Caddy Eldorado bellowing The Theme ka-wumphs up the ramp into Harry's parking lot and squeals to a stop. Then Cadillac No. 2, Cadillac No. 3 and Cadillac No. 4, all second-hand Eldorados polished beyond dazzle. The golfers park the cars precisely next to each other like a flotilla of battleships and, in sloppy unison, loose one last blast of The Theme.

"They're here!" says Koko.

Into the restaurant struts the most magnificent foursome since the court of Louis XVI. Their sartorial splendor varies in intensity from week to week, but it's always enough to floor Koko, who has ushered at Puerto Rican weddings.

This particular Sunday, the fat Kloppman twins, Leo and Leon, known as Tweedledee and Tweedledum, featured pink knickers with big yellow polka dots, and yellow Italian-mesh shirts with lots of chest-hair sticking through. Little Abe Schurz wore a Royal Stewart plaid jumpsuit. And Roy-goy Feldman was in a white-on-white bush jacket with candy-striped slacks. His silver golf cap was tilted at a 45-degree angle. Roy-goy's real name was Leroy, but his friends called him Roy-goy because with his chiseled features, he looked like a member of the House of Lords. Roy-goy Feldman made Rex Harrison look like a door-to-door blintz peddler.

"Tacos!" yelled Tweedledee. But Koko already had the cauldron bubbling. The pungent, new smell of onion, garlic, chopped beef and chili peppers joined the old standbys, used grease and fresh Lysol, creating a whole new mood. The foursome would demolish a dozen and a half tacos and wash them down with at least a gallon of bright artificial orange drink.

With the tacos cooking and the comments on the costumes out of the way ("You look like second runner-up at the 1938 Annual Fag Picnic"), Tweedledum spread several maps over three tables, two chairs, the main counter and the checkout counter. The maps pointed up the purpose of the whole rendezvous. Harry's Hamburgatorium was the staging point, the nerve center, the strategy room where the golfers would make the critical decision of just where to play their weekly match.

And what a cut-throat match. What action. Basically, a quarter a hole, every man for himself, one-tie, all-tie. Basically also, a buck Nassau. Presses on either or both situations to be invoked at the discretion of early losers: hand in hand went basho, trappo, splasho, boundo, bingo, bango, bungo. Basho was the longest drive; trappo, every trap entered cost a quarter to all; splasho, every water hazard entered cost a quarter to all; boundo, every shot out-of-bounds cost a quarter to all. Bingo, bango and bungo were, of course, first on, closest to the hole and first in, and, like basho, garnered a quarter from all. To add spice: a buck a par, five bucks for a birdie, a grand for an eagle, and five grand for a hole-in-one. The last two categories were as yet unachieved, although Abe Schurz almost knocked in an 8-iron on a short par-3 two years earlier at a course deep in northern Pennsylvania. Abe was barely a scorecard and a half from $15,000. To top off all this action was the team play-best ball match. Losers buy the beer and gas. Because the players all handicapped out around 20, teams were assigned strictly on a rotating basis. If everything went wrong, a golfer could lose thousands of dollars or, with all the breaks, win a fortune. It always came out pretty close to a dead heat.

The match was a delicious nerve wrack, but the big problem was where to play it. New York City golfers and the nearby golf courses constitute a vast blivet: too many golfers and not enough courses. Serious golfers are victims of both the population explosion and the new deification of the professional golfer. The press worships so abjectly at the shrines of Palmer, Nicklaus, Trevino and Miller that the game has become a national craze. If you aren't swinging the sticks you are nowhere. Result: nowhere to swing the sticks. The only possible solution is to go both early and far. The foursome had ranged hundreds of miles from the city. They had probed the wilds of New Jersey, the Finger Lakes of upstate New York and the back country of Connecticut, even Massachusetts and Vermont, in search of freedom from crowds and peace of hitting. But what a will-o-the-wisp. There was something wrong with everywhere.

The golfers swaggered around Harry's from map to map, like generals at an underground war ministry. Gesturing with tacos instead of swagger sticks, and with brows furrowed in concentration, they discussed the possibilities.

"Pocahontas!" said Abe pointing at a town on a map stained with the taco juice and orange drink of countless Sunday mornings. "Let's go back to Pocahontas."

"Pocahontas-schmontas!" said Roy-goy.

"You know what's happened to Pocahontas? A new GE plant. I've got a client who says Pocahontas has turned into Coney Island."

"How about Twin-Lakes?" said Tweedledee. "I have positive memories of Twin-Lakes."

"That's because you like fat ladies," said Tweedledum. "There are more fat ladies at Twin-Lakes than in the stylish-stout section of Bloomingdale's basement. We were stuck behind nine foursomes, all fat, and not one of those blobs ever got the ball off the ground."

Abe Schurz chugged his third orange drink with his left hand while probing a map with his right forefinger.

"Hey, guys. We played this little town, Montrose, one time. Right here, look, sort of in the Catskills. What's wrong with Montrose?"

The golfers crowded around Abe's map.

"I remember what's wrong with Montrose," said Tweedledum, "Binghamton. The entire population of Binghamton plays golf at Montrose."

"That's right," said Roy-goy, "and half of Scranton. Montrose took third or maybe even second in our Crowded-Course-of-the-Year nominations."

The discussions raged from map to map and Koko kept the tacos and orange drinks coming.

The golfers were buddies from way back. They all went to Horace Mann High School and NYU. They were all CPA's and they all lived in the Bronx. Of the four, only Roy-goy was unmarried. And Roy-goy was different in another way, too. He was rich. Roy-goy had read somewhere that all of America's great fortunes were made because someone in the family took the available funds and shot craps with them. Roy-goy had a series of crap shoots that all worked. It was the era of the hot new issue. Roy-goy would get in, ride it up, get out, and then shoot the whole bundle on the next one. He never copped his bet. And in that five-year glory period, Roy-goy Feldman piled up more than $8 million. None of his friends knew a thing about it.

Roy-goy sent heavy farm equipment to a kibbutz in Israel on a continuing basis, and he endowed a perpetual scholarship at NYU. But he had no personal desires that involved large sums of money. The only real hangnail in his life was crowded golf courses. And Roy-goy couldn't seem to solve the problem.

There were several things wrong with the private clubs in the area. First, they featured something no real golfer could stand the sight of: that mincing, priggish, little sissy dressed in white, the tennis player. Second, there was a whole mushy welter of irrelevant activity: swimming, bridge and family-oriented eating. Third, they allowed women on the golf course with ever-increasing frequency, even granted them special hours and days for play.

Most important of all, the private clubs seemed even more jammed than the public courses. As a guest, Roy-goy had played several seven-hour rounds at supposedly exclusive country clubs.

One solution was simply to buy a golf course for his own private use. After a particularly frustrating Sunday morning journey to a crowded nowhere, Roy-goy went down and inspected a golf course for sale near the Jersey shore. It was flat and almost tree-less, cost $3 million and required a 12-man maintenance crew plus unbelievable amounts of water, fertilizer and grass seed. Roy-goy returned to the city, beaten.

Abe Schurz's eyes widened in excitement. "Come here, you guys!" he shouted. "Look what I found!"

The others crowded around as Abe pointed at a tiny flag near the center of Pennsylvania.

"That flag means golf course," said Abe.

"And there's nothing near it," said Roy-goy.

"Look at those hashmarks all around it," said Tweedledee. "They mean mountains."

Tweedledum was skeptical.

"A golf course in the mountains with nothing near it? Not even a town? Not even a main road? And it has no name so nobody can even call it. It's too good to be true."

"Look!" said Roy-goy pointing with his fourth taco. "It's too far for Pittsburgh, too far for Harrisburg, way too far for Philly."

"Too far for anywhere in Jersey," said Tweedledee, "and certainly too far for any sane person in New York."

"Guys," said Abe Schurz almost reverently, "we deserve this little flag. We've been searching for our Garden of Eden for almost 14 years and we've finally found it. Let's roll!"

The foursome always used Schurz's metallic green Eldorado. At one time they flipped for who drove, but Schurz always lost, so they just naturally piled into his car. After four solid hours on the road they all sensed that something weird was happening. The farther they got from the city, the heavier the traffic seemed to be. On hills, the stream of lights stretched out from horizon to horizon.

"Hey!" said Abe Schurz, "that car that just passed us was Tex Lieberman and the golfers that meet at Merv's Bowling Alley."

"What's happening?" said Tweedledum.

"What's happening," said Roy-goy, "is that every wisenheimer on the Eastern Seaboard sat somewhere with maps and sliderules and figured out that the little flag with the hashmarks around it was the one place to go where nobody would be."

It was a colossal coincidence arrived at by animal instinct, trained minds and pure logic. And this great stream of cars was only one of three bumper-to-bumper caravan hordes converging on an isolated mountain hamlet. Traffic staggered to a stop. Three winking Mars lights moved slowly along the opposite lane as sheriff's police tried to fathom the phenomenon. As dawn broke, the lead squad car stopped opposite the foursome and two policemen got out. They flashed lights into the front and back seats.

"You fellas sure you're not rock musicians?"

"Do we look like rock musicians?" said Tweedledum angrily.

The policeman studied Tweedledum's polka dot knickers and Italian mesh shirt. He shook his head in wonderment.

"That's hard to say. But I've read about them rock concerts. Smoking pot, taking all their clothes off, messing up the place. We don't want that kind of thing around here. You fellows ain't hiding any marijuana, are you?"

"Look here, officer," said Abe Schurz, "we are golfers. And we have traveled a great distance to play golf near here."

The policeman turned to his partner.

"Hear that, Ox? These fellas come for golf, too."

He turned back to the foursome.

"They used to have a little 9-hole golf course up near the reservoir. Turned it back into a pasture 10 or 12 years ago."

Abe Schurz was infuriated.

"Then why do they still have the flag on the map?"

Abe thrust the map at him and pointed out the flag.

"Must be an old map," said the policeman "or maybe nobody told the map people to take it off. On or off, there ain't no golf here."

Cars up ahead began backing and turning and heading back where they came from. Dawn had broken over the pastoral countryside of central Pennsylvania. On the left was a great barn with a large hex sign on the side. A herd of Holsteins lined a fence and stared in amazement at the colorful carloads of angry golfers.

The policeman held up traffic and motioned Abe into a "U" turn. The foursome began the trek back.

As the Eldorado crossed the New Jersey line, Roy-goy was curled up in a ball half asleep with his face pressed against the cool glass of the side window. His mouth and nose were open, his pale blue eyes, half-lidded, stared dazedly at gentleman farms, populated with pasture after pasture of Holstein cows (your *only* Jewish cow, he mused).

Roy-goy closed his eyes and dreamed a wonderful dream of an emerald and velvet golf course with snowy white traps and gleaming ponds. Scarlet flags gently stirred hither and thither. This utopia had the ultimate gift: no people. As the lush fairways, doglegs, water holes and trap-ringed greens floated by on Roy-goy's dream tour, he saw perhaps one twosome. No labor-rally horde at the first tee. No number, no arguing, no shoving, no pre-dawn tee-offs, no lost balls. No bogged, clogged 22-minute waits while the miserable swine on the green lined up 10-inch putts. No Asiatic fivesomes moving in slow motion as if in a tea ceremony. No fat ladies, no skinny ladies. No hassle. Just click and go.

Roy-goy opened his eyes and stared into the faces of

an awestricken farm family less than a foot away as Abe passed their churchbound Dodge. And Roy-goy accepted for a moment that Panacea Country Club only existed in his mind. But then he saw the end of it through the dirty Dodge window. Unmistakably, a tee with blue, white and red markers.

"Stop the car!" he shouted.

Abe Schurz took a moment to vacate an angry, muttering, gesturing reverie of his own. "What, stop the car?" he demanded.

"Stop the car," said Roy-goy.

They pulled over at a picnic stand. Tweedledum and Tweedledee snored on.

'What's that golf club back there?"

Abe had been so busy chastising the top management of his firm that he didn't know exactly where he was. His pale little eyes stabbed like lasers through the surrounding countryside.

"We're in Qwinkle. You notice how it all looks slightly fake? Qwinkle."

"Qwinkle? There's a golf course back there with nobody on it at 11 o'clock Sunday morning. Qwinkle? You're putting me on."

"Qwinkle is named after the cereal guy. Qwinkle Golf only has 50 members, no broads, no guests allowed. These guys are all Chairmen of the Board of something. The 50 split up the costs every year. Runs like 17 big ones apiece. There was an article about it a couple of months ago."

"WASP?"

"Qwinkle is so WASP even a WASP can't get in."

"Where do they live? Is there a town?"

"There's Qwinkle—100-acre farms with horses, pools, courts, greenhouses, antiques, tractors to ride around on, Mercedes to go to market. What can I tell you? Read the article."

When they got back to the Bronx, Roy-goy knew exactly what to do. He called the office, his broker, his lawyer, packed and caught the evening jet for London. As he floated through the stratosphere, his thoughts wandered along the incredible green fairways of the impossible people-free golf course that really existed.

Roy-goy's London solicitor, himself a golfer, was amused at the discovery of Qwinkle, but incredulous at the solution to the problem.

"Mr. Feldman, it won't work."

"Look, Mr. Brearly," said Roy-goy, "I don't blame you for not understanding this, because it's so dumb. But it's true. The richer Americans get, the more British they try to be. British cars, British clothes, British-looking houses, British accents. Back in the 20's it was the ambition of every rich mother to have her daughter marry a titled Englishman.

"Mr. Brearly, I'm a Jew. That makes it impossible for me to join Qwinkle or any other non-Jewish club. And even if I were a rich WASP-American it would take me years, maybe forever to join Qwinkle Golf. As a titled Englishman, I think 72 hours will do it. Now first, what's my name?"

Brearly lighted his pipe and walked over to an antique crony bar. He indicated the cut glass decanters of sherry and port. He was warming to this bizarre assignment. He poured two drinks and handed one to Roy-goy.

"Well, I would hold on to Roy somehow. After all, it does mean *King*. I have it—Fitzroy. That means 'bastard son of.' Somewhere back in history, a dallying king produced one of your forebears."

Roy-goy held up his glass and nodded. "Fitzroy. I like it. Fitzroy. With a hyphen?"

"If you wish. Fitz-Roy. Let's go with a hyphen."

"All right now," said Roy-goy, "Fitz-Roy what?"

Brearly looked out the massive mullioned window at the Thames. Across the river through the mist rose the houses of Parliament and Westminster Abbey. He turned and looked at Roy-goy.

"The name must be very British, very historical. How about Hampton?"

"He's a jazz musician in America."

"Plantagenet?"

43

"Too hard to pronounce."

"Tudor?"

"That's a car with two doors."

"Wellington?"

"Wellington! Fitz-Roy Wellington! Sir Fitz-Roy Wellington! That will flatten them."

Brearly wagged his finger.

"Feldman, the title is on you. I take no responsibility."

"Brearly, my good man," said Roy-goy, affecting a British accent, "the title is our little secret. Place the call."

It was 8:00 p.m. London time, making it 2:00 in Pennsylvania. Joe Farnsworth, the fat, ruddy proprietor of Qwinkle Properties, was busy putting on the oriental rug in his office in the historic stone silo his father had converted to headquarter the real estate company. Farnsworth was an Ivy League flunkout who had tried Wall Street and then joined Father. The qualities he most admired in people were: money, ostentation and rudeness. Bullying waiters was his favorite sport next to golf. And he liked to spend hot summer afternoons sitting by the club pool, wearing dark glasses so he could get away with ogling his friends' teenage daughters. Farnsworth was an elder in the Qwinkle Congregational Church, and Qwinkle's prime gatekeeper. Farnsworth could discourage the "wrong kind" of people. He hit a perfect putt into the center of the electric ball-return device, and let out a guttural yell of victory as he punched his right fist forward. The phone rang.

"Qwinkle Properties, Farnsworth speaking."

"This is Maxwell Brearly calling from London . . . ."

"London, England?"

"London, England. I represent Sir Fitz-Roy Wellington, who has authorized me to purchase him a property in Qwinkle."

"In Qwinkle? There is nothing available right in Qwinkle, and I don't expect there will be for a year or so. But we are developing some beautiful land over near the Spingpang River . . ."

"Mr. Farnsworth," said Brearly, "the property must be

in Qwinkle proper and must be substantial, pleasant and with acreage."

Farnsworth bounced a golf ball off the rock wall of the silo.

"What can I tell you, Brearly? Qwinkle is very exclusive. You can't just pick up the phone and move in . . . ."

"Look, Farnsworth, I can easily get a list of the property owners in Qwinkle and make a direct deal. I'm calling you because you're there. *You* do it! Sir Fitz-Roy is impatient. He wants this wrapped up fast."

Farnsworth bounced the ball and then grinned and stuck out his tongue as an idea occurred.

"Listen, Brearly, there's my own estate."

"Describe it."

"One hundred and fifteen acres, pond, creek, the usual pre-Revolutionary War house brought all the way up, country kitchen, lots of original paneling and hardware, six bedrooms, five and a half baths, barn, stables, greenhouse, swimming pool, interiors by Sophie Blattner, everything freshly painted, mint condition."

"Is there anything better?"

"Better? My place is the best estate here! People drive in just to see it. It's been in *House Lovely*. What do you mean, 'better'?"

Brearly was patient but firm.

"Look here, Farnsworth. Lord Wellington wears a gold buckle with a 20-karat ruby in it. It was presented to his great-grandfather by Empress Eugenie. The Wellington family today owns 1/24th of England. Why, if it weren't for the Iron Duke at Waterloo, you would likely be in a French penal institution today. Let me be direct. You have just described to me a shack, a habitation fit for a goat farmer. But no matter. It will have to do. What is the price?"

Farnsworth bounced the ball. The going price for his place, whether in Qwinkle or elsewhere in the countryside was about $200,000.

"I couldn't let it go for a penny less than half a million."

"Done!" said Brearly. "But there is a contingency."

"A contingency?" said Farnsworth. "A mortgage contingency?"

"Don't be an idiot, Farnsworth. The contingency is membership in Qwinkle Golf."

Farnsworth stopped bouncing the ball, his eyes widened in alarm. "Impossible."

"We are betting half a million you can do it."

"Membership in Qwinkle Golf is handed down from father to son. The only reason I'm a member is because my grandfather was one of the founders."

"Half a million cash and a famous British lord. Think of it as the opportunity of a lifetime for both you and the club."

Farnsworth's face screwed up in concentration.

"When do I get the earnest money? I need 10 percent down."

"Don't be silly! You'll receive the full price by cable, immediately. But get cracking on the contingency, Farnsworth. It is now 2:19 Eastern daylight time. In precisely 48 hours, the deal is dead."

When it came to a buck, Farnsworth could move his chubby body with surprising speed. He made three brief phone calls and then roared out to Bobby Champ's farm where the entire board of directors of Qwinkle Golf was shooting skeet. Roy-goy was right. The British mystique knocked them flat.

"Sir Fitz-Roy Wellington? He was an ace in World War II. Flew a Spitfire, I believe," said Bobby. "We're lucky to get him."

Tall, bald Harrison Patterson nodded sagely.

"Right you are, Bobby, and he's a director of literally dozens of British companies. I met him one time at a party at the Dorchester. He probably wouldn't remember me. Marvelous fellow. Of course, we'll extend membership."

Toadlike Harold Huff was puzzled. "And he's already purchased property here? Why did he choose Qwinkle?"

Farnsworth smiled and held out his hands, palms up. "Lord Wellington said Qwinkle is the most charming place he has ever seen."

They voted on the spot, and Roy-goy Feldman became a member of perhaps the most exclusive club in America.

Only a Brittania jet was big enough to accommodate the Rolls Corniche roadster. Roy-goy had it shipped to New York complete with British plates and the Wellington coat of arms on both doors. He arrived at Kennedy Friday night and checked into an airport hotel. He picked up the car the next morning and headed for Qwinkle.

Qwinkles are America's favorite breakfast cereal, and people can't believe there was actually a man named Qwinkle, any more than they believe there was a man named Birdseye who pioneered frozen food. Old Clyde Qwinkle figured out how to explode a peanut back in 1882, and Qwinkles have been on America's breakfast table ever since.

The 75-room Qwinkle mansion was destroyed by fire in 1900. The carriage house survived and became the Qwinkle Golf Clubhouse, a handsome Victorian structure made of narrow clapboard, featuring a series of large round windows with ornate intersticing. The eaves are heavily gingerbreaded and the long, peaked roof is topped with three martin house cupolas with lightning rod weathervanes. The balustraded veranda was added after World War I. The three men waiting on the veranda stiffened as Roy-goy's Rolls entered the parking lot.

Roy-goy wheeled over to the only other car in the lot, slammed on the brakes, and inadvertently hit the horn which produced a metallic squawk. The men on the veranda nervously waved. It was a different Roy-goy. As Sir Fitz-Roy Wellington, his longish hair was cropped like Hamlet, sideburns gone. Also gone were the crazy clothes. Lord Wellington wore black from cap to shoes. And, of course, the heirloom belt buckle Brearly had told Farnsworth about. It was actually brass and glass and had been purchased by Brearly in a junk shop in Chelsea. He had improvised the Empress Eugenie story on the phone. Roy-goy noticed that all three men stared at the buckle. The "ruby" winked at them.

The luncheon was filet mignon and Chateau Lafitte in-

47

stead of tacos and orange drink. Harrison Patterson gave a monologue about the historic ties between Britain and the United States. Roy-goy responded with his views on British peerage. He felt it was dreadfully undemocratic to be born to wealth and a title. He would certainly welcome the day he became just plain Fitz-Roy Wellington. He told a few coronation jokes and some rumors about what really goes on at Buckingham Palace.

Roy-goy had a gnawing feeling all through lunch that legions of golfers were arriving and stacking up on the first tee. But there was nobody there but the four caddies, and still only two cars in the parking lot.

It was a flawless round of golf. Not a cloud in the sky, not a puff of wind. The fairways were a deep, rich green, closely cropped and without a weed. The ball sat up in perpetual winter rule. And it clicked off the clubs and seemed to ride against the sky in slow motion.

There was no unsportsmanlike sneezing during backswings. No finger jinxes or X's drawn between the ball and the cup. There was no derisive laughter. No gloating over a lucky shot or cursing over a bad bounce. There was no ridiculous clutter of bets, just a gentlemanly 50¢ Nassau. And everybody played straight, safe, and sure—what Roy-goy called geezer golf. Shoot for the center of the green, lay up in front of any water and every first putt is a Ginsberg. Make-sense golf, quiet, refined, dignified. Not a single, solitary soul on the entire course outside of their group. Incredible.

After holing out on 18, they returned to the veranda for Qwinkle juleps.

Roy-goy looked at his watch and stood up.

"Bligh me! It's past tea time, I have to run," he said.

"See you tomorrow, Sir Fitz-Roy?" said Harrison Patterson.

"Same time, same station, Lord Wellington?" said Bobby Champ.

"Tomorrow it's Camp David in the morning and then I race the sun to Hong Kong. Ta ta! boys."

"Ta ta! Lord," they chorused. "Cheerio!"

Roy-goy rammed the Rolls into gear, spun gravel and raced down the country road to Farnsworth's Farm. He skidded into the entranceway, clipping the iron jockey and barely missing the colonial coachlight. At the end of the long driveway the two big vans still straddled the turnaround as they swallowed up Farnsworth's antiques. Roy-goy drove past the courts and the pool and parked the Rolls in the barn. A fat Palomino in a box stall stared at him like a goldfish.

Roy-goy jogged past the house and out the drive. It was hot and he was sweating long before he completed the mile and a half to Qwinkle Crossroads. When he arrived he bought a cherry Popsicle at Ye Country Store and sprawled on the bus stop bench. Roy-goy couldn't believe Qwinkle. Everything was white clapboard, black shutters and red geraniums. Even the gas stations, the supermarket, the movie theatre. And there were only two kinds of cars: Mercedes sedans and Volvo station wagons. Roy-goy took the bus to Newark, hopped a train to New York and a subway to the Bronx. Back in his apartment he poured himself a Dad's Old Fashioned and picked up the phone.

"Farnsworth, old boy? Lord Wellington here. Three things: one, I don't like the estate, as you call it. Sell it for what you can get. Two, Qwinkle Golf doesn't suit me, and the members are rum. I quit. Three, the Rolls. You keep it. The signed title is in the glove tray. Deal with Brearly in London. Ta-ta!" He hung up the phone.

The next morning at about 3:00, Roy-goy put on a pair of fake lizard-skin pants and a gold shirt, hit the street in his Eldorado and blared up the "River Kwai" theme on the air horns. Minutes later he ka-whumpfed into Harry's parking lot and squealed to a stop next to Tweedledee Kloppman. They exchanged Groucho Marx-style eyebrow action.

Ka-wumpf! came Abe Schurz.

Ka-wumpf! came Tweedledum.

Schurz held up one finger dramatically, and then dropped it. For the first time ever, the foursome hit the theme in perfect unison.

THE LOWEST
ROUND ON RECORD

Herbert Huppman's fabulous round of 47, fashioned in the New Zealand Amateur of 1927, is one of those records that will never be beaten.

Huppman, an inhabitant of Tasmania where he ran a ski wax factory, became a golfing enthusiast solely through his interest in things financial. A tycoon of no small account, Huppman, in addition to owning the big ski wax works, also dabbled in taxidermy, copra and the manufacture of stilts.

An ardent reader of various financial journals, he was continually encountering the name Rockefeller, which seemed to be synonymous with success. Striving to emulate this industrial giant, Herbert took to tipping with shiny new tuppences (much to the annoyance of Tasmanian servitors), and to the game of golf, a phenomenon hitherto unknown within a thousand miles.

Huppman laid out a short, crude nine-hole course in Tasmania's Mt. Bischoff region and using ancient equipment which had been brought to the island by his great-great-grandfather more than a century earlier, soon became the best and only golfer in the country. Because of his affluence and influence he was always "Mr. Huppman" or "Bossman" to his face, but behind his back the natives began referring to him as "Subgummo," which means "Crazy Herb" in Tasmanian. Golf was to the Tasmanians somewhat incomprehensible.

Since the only picture he had ever seen of Rockefeller showed the great John D. wearing an Inverness Cape, Herb adopted this accoutrement as part of his golf garb. In action the Inverness, coupled with a highly unorthodox swing style, gave him the appearance of a crippled crow. Huppman's prominent beak did nothing to dispel this illusion.

Craving competition of any caliber, but continuing to

snub Australia due to its preposterous import tax on ski wax, Herbert Huppman read with unfeigned interest of the coming New Zealand Amateur. He made application and then retired to his Mt. Bischoff layout for some final practice.

The New Zealand Amateur is handled in much the same ways as the U.S. Amateur. Regional qualifying rounds are played, with the cream of the regional crops meeting in match play. As Huppman was the entire Tasmanian crop, and his entry blank indicated that he was regularly shooting in the high 60's, he automatically qualified.

The first hole measured 128 yards. Huppman selected one of his ancient relics carved from a solid piece of wood. (His clubs were all of this archaic type and he carried them loose, never having heard of either a caddie or bag). He assumed a grotesque "sit down" stance at the ball (apparently gleaned from the few photographs he had ever seen of a golf swing), took an indescribably awkward cut which seemed to be a cross between a field hockey and cricket stroke, and sent the ball bounding with plenty of top spin, down the fairway. It wended its way between traps, neatly avoided a gleaming tarn, leaped the final bunker, slammed into the pin, hesitated and dropped. The gallery roared its approval and forsaking McPhee, Kronstadtler, Malenkov, and other big names, joined the Tasmanian clouter.

It soon became apparent, however, that this was not Huppman's regular game—that his hole-in-one, in fact, had been purely a matter of chance. For while his golf continued in the same vein, with the ball never leaving the ground, the results definitely did not. There were no more holes-in-one or anything even faintly approaching them. His bounders all began to find every hazard on the course.

And then another unique feature of the Tasmanian's game came to light. Herbert often had to take two or three swipes at the ball before connecting solidly, but it soon became apparent that he had no idea that these counted (explaining in part perhaps, along with the shortness of the course, his scores in the 60's at home). When informed of this scoring technicality, Huppman launched a shattering tirade against the official, a mild mannered man named Broon, and was placated only when confronted with the rule book.

But the situation continued to deteriorate. The bounders came to worse and worse grief, the whiffs became increasingly plentiful.

Herbert's Inverness wilted, until he took on the appearance of a vexed vulture. He spent a good portion of his time heaping imprecations on poor Broon, and when the final divot had been dug, signed his card with an oath and returned to the clubhouse veranda for a gin and bitters.

It was then that a big hullabaloo broke out in the Limehouse Links committee room. It seemed that poor distracted Broon, after adding Herbert's card, had left the 1 out of the 147 total and signed the card. Under NZGA rules the score had to stand, unless the player disqualified himself. When the delegation found a slightly pickled Herbert Huppman they told him the story and implored him to do the only honorable thing. Herbert looked from grim face to grim face, roared with laughter and told them to go to hell. Broon fainted.

And so it was that Herbert Huppman's 47 became official. The first round of match play, though noteworthy, was really anti-climactic. Herbert was paired with a cobbler's son named Mawk and was beaten 19 and 17, though Mawk shot straight bogeys. Herbert cared little and spent the remaining days on the veranda.

At the Championship dinner he smiled at the cat-calls and hisses and graciously accepted the ornate medalist's cup. The next day he set sail for Tasmania and was never again seen in golfing circles.

BEST TERRIER, FASTEST GIRL

They stood on the first tee smoking Tiparillos. The little orange glows as they sucked on the plastic mouthpieces underlined how dark it was. Not dawn. No faint light in the east heralding morning. Just black dark.

"I've got a snowy-white Titleist here that's going to break your heart all day," said Wilmarth.

"I'm going with the only truly Jewish golf ball," said Bernardi.

"Maxfli!" They warbled in unison.

"Where is that pigeon?" said Bernardi. "He's going to really screw us up in about four minutes."

They both looked toward the parking lot. Reber was late, and at least three cars had arrived one after the other, headlights cutting out bushes and trees before leaping back to dark. Now a pale glow in the east definitely established itself. Paler and stronger than the orange, electric-light glow of Chicago 21 miles south. It was nervous time on the tee. If you're first off, you go off just before it's humanly possible to see either the ball or where it's supposed to go. And either you go off when you're told or you relinquish your position.

"Where is that Reber, that biter?" said Bernardi.

"You know who's behind us?" said Wilmarth. "The Japs. Must be 15 or 20 of them. And I think I saw Harold Sims."

Both of these bits of news terrorized Bernardi. A large group of Japanese out of the city had discovered Elmwood Golf Club, and playing behind them was exquisite torture. They played fivesomes with the approval of the Elmwood starter. And they were as lousy as they were cool-looking. They all had off-balance, chopping, scooping, Samurai-sword swings that resulted in little pop flies. They were deadly slow and unaware of the idea of letting someone through.

Harold Sims was something else. Whereas Wilmarth, Bernardi and Reber hit quick and walked fast, Sims had a grating ritual. He tossed grass in the air not once but twice. Especially if the weather was dead calm. Then he would walk 20 or 30 yards up toward the hole, squint at it and then stand or squat for as long as a minute deciding God knows what. Then he'd return and methodically select a club, swing it four times before discovering it was the wrong club. After selecting a new one and swinging *it* four times, he'd hit. And this was the most irritating part of all: his hit would generally end up maybe four feet from the cup. The group had been saddled with big, strong, moon-faced Harold Sims twice. He added a full hour and a half to their usual three-hour round.

"Here's Reber," said Bernardi, "I'll tee up."

Reber, with his white visor, his red alpaca, his tartan slacks and his four-toned golf shoes, threaded his way through the Japanese patrol to the tee.

"Jesus, Reeb," said Wilmarth, "one more frigging minute and we're somewhere between Fujiyama and the Ginza."

"Did you bring the trophy?" said Bernardi.

"Look at this gorgiosa!" said Reber, holding it up. "An actual-size gold bowling ball flanked by two actual-size pins. This sucker has to weigh 20 pounds."

"What's it say on it?" said Wilmarth.

The raspy public address speaker let out a feed-back scream and then spoke.

"Wilmarth, Bernardi, Reber, go!"

"It says, 'Abernathy Screw Machine—Second Place.' I'll leave it with the starter."

The threesome drove off into the dark green world as thousands of shafts of pastel-colored sunlight poked their way through the forest preserve bordering the east side of the course. The three carts made drunken trails through the heavy dew.

Trophies were an important part of Saturday morning golf. They were a joke but they were serious. None of the threesome had ever been a real athlete, so none had ever won anything. Bringing home a trophy for beating two other guys wasn't much, but it did make you a winner. On top of that, a bunch of trophies gave off an osmotic patina of athletic prowess that was never questioned. Trophies and cups high on shelves are unreadable. A guest just accepts all that excellence.

Bernardi started it with a magnificent trophy purchased at a church rummage sale for 75 cents. It was an amazing concoction of brass and marble surmounted by a faceless couple grappling with each other. The plaque said, "Peoria Waltz Festival, 1939. H & D Zimmerman."

Wilmarth won it by chipping in on the 18th, and the following week put up what appeared to be a silver crematorium urn. It had a fake onyx base and a statue of Winged Victory holding an olive wreath on the top. A Spencerian script read, "Best Terrier, Mason City, 1954. Donated by the Amalgamated Bank." It cost Wilmarth a dollar at the Goodwill.

Bernardi took it home after an onslaught that closed both Reber and Wilmarth out on the 14th. Bernardi's 77 was his round of the year.

Every week during the summer the previous week's winner put up some kind of a trophy for the coming week's match. There were only two guidelines: the trophy must be grandiose and it must have nothing to do with golf. These factors forced the concept into a farce, legitimized it. But Bernardi carried it too far. While Reber and Wilmarth came up with normal to splendid trophies and loving cups, Bernardi went strictly for the absurd. He unearthed three trophies at a house sale that had gold chickens as the focus. He found trophies for knitting, salesmanship, canasta, cooking and cat shows. And he found many trophies for female athletic events: diving, volleyball, field hockey and free-throw shooting with appropriate figurines featured.

Reber and Wilmarth would shake their heads and whoop in glee over the Bernardi trophies. But they secretly hated them and whenever each received one, he would not take it home. The Bernardi trophies, like many murder guns, often ended up in secluded culverts.

Bernardi's all-time favorite trophy featured a large, crouching Indian girl who looked Chinese and had no ears. Big block letters read, "Fastest Girl, Camp Mohican, Field Day—1947." He found this gem at a moving and storage company unclaimed goods store for a quarter. He had to own it but he felt he had to win it. So he put it up one Saturday when Reber was out of town. And he proudly took "Fastest Girl" home after beating Wilmarth one up, even though Bernardi knew Wilmarth blew a two-foot putt to *avoid* winning the monstrosity, and Wilmarth knew that Bernardi knew he blew it for that reason.

The golfers arrived at Bernardi's ball first. He hit a 4-iron on a line two feet off the ground. It bounced along with a rooster tail of dew, ran through a trap and rolled up to within a foot of the flag.

"Christ!" said Wilmarth.

"I knew there was no lip there," said Bernardi with a sweet smile.

When they got to Wilmarth's ball it was 6-iron range. He hung a high shot out to the right.

"Go left, you prong!" he yelled.

It hit the side of the bank and dove for the right rough. Wilmarth's chubby face was red with rage. He took four slow practice swings, none of which had any relationship to his real swing.

The threesome trudged on now in quest of Reber's drive. They automatically veered right and then farther and farther right. The ball was a foot from the drainage ditch that bordered the forest preserve, some 290 yards off the tee, 100 yards right of the fairway. How a drive could be so far off line was one of the world's great Saturday morning mysteries.

Reber was an immense, shambling, pigeon-toed person who had a bovine, simple-minded look that belied his position as a brilliant research chemist. He was a shy, withdrawn man, a loner who played golf as a single until the day he hooked up with Bernardi and Wilmarth.

Reber had a big, upright swing with full extension; a

smooth, rhythmic, inside-out swing with plenty of wrist; great contact, the clubhead hitting the ball with a classic click. Reber also had positively the worst slice in the history of golf. The ball seemed to flee to the right even before being hit. There was no way to dignify this crazy, roundhouse swoop with words like "push" or "fade." Somehow the ball became a maddened boomerang as it soared out of sight over trees, billboards and Good Humor trucks.

Wilmarth and Bernardi would crouch, baffled, behind this paragon swing, looking for the fatal flaw. Nothing. It was Sam Snead perfect. After trying everything from hooding, to crushing with the right hand, to using the other players' clubs, Reber gave up and resorted to playing the ball some 45 degrees left. Even so, the ball would often fly all the way around and into the right rough or worse. And when it did, quiet introspective Reber could be heard to mutter this word:

"Fuckleheimer."

Reber's affliction vanished when he hit irons. He lined up and predictably nailed a perfectly straight 6-iron—170 yards long and a mile high—15 feet from the can. Same swing, never a slice. Very mysterious.

While Reber was always natty in alligator shirts, Daks and Footjoys, Wilmarth wore faded and patched World War II army fatigues, with the pants secured below his jiggling tummy. His hair looked like Little Orphan Annie's and he had yellow buck teeth and a breath that caused birds to swerve in flight. He also wore thick glasses that made his cat-green eyes look the size of poker chips.

Wilmarth was the best golfer of the threesome and the worst cheater. He had two special tricks Reber and Bernardi were on to. On the green he would always mark the front or hole side of the ball, and then replace it as if he had marked the back of the ball. This gained him two inches. In disaster areas, unless you stuck pretty close to Wilmarth, any out-of-bounds or unplayable shot never was. Lo! It was always in the clear with an open shot to the green. The only solid evidence of this gambit was that Wilmarth often ran out of golf balls. He also unabashedly teed the ball up in the rough with his clubhead. Reber and Bernardi only did so if they had a bad lie.

Wilmarth was also a counter. When asked what he got on a hole, he would feign puzzlement, turn back toward the hole and, pointing with index finger, count each blow. This tactic naturally disincorporated all dubs.

At the first green, Wilmarth hit the pin with a skulled chip that dropped. Reber rimmed the cup and said, "Fuckleheimer." Bernardi got his bird with a tap-in. A par and two birdies made up of bad shots and miracles, the long-time pattern of the threesome.

And the miracles continued. Reber's incredible banana ball on two accelerated through a six-inch slot between two giant birch trees, circled over a duck pond and plopped down in the center of the proper fairway. His approach was stony. Bernardi smother-hooked two woods and then sank a 4-iron. Wilmarth hit three long bounders and then canned an 88-footer. And as the sun cleared the woods, a few good shots plus minor cheating and the big widemouthed smile of good fortune had the threesome making the turn at just two over par.

What each golfer didn't know was that part of this extraordinary scoring was plain old-fashioned determination. Each hungered to have the incredible golden bowling trophy for his own, and for very different reasons.

Reber had fallen in love with its glittering bulk upon first spotting it surrounded by elderly ski boots at the church rummage sale. It was all the trophies he'd ever seen presented to others, at school assemblies and on the tube. "Gosh!" he said to himself humbly and as if to a nationwide audience, "I want to thank my mom and dad, my coach, and all the guys on the team. I couldn't have done it without them."

For Wilmarth the trophy filled in a glaring chink in his false all-around athleticism. Wilmarth had phony trophies for archery, lacrosse, bumper pool, boccie ball, shuffleboard, rummy and dressage. Bowling gave him a new and very masculine dimension.

Bernardi had almost shrieked when he saw the trophy,

just for its outstanding all-American grossness. But it was more. The concoction almost belonged in the Museum of Modern Art.

At the end of No. 12, the threesome was deadlocked at four over. Bernardi was the first to go. His drive on 13 caught the Gobi, a large and deep sand trap with a great lip. Bernardi took four swipes with a sand wedge, each swipe causing the ball to run up and inspect the lip, then return precisely to its former position. Bernardi then went completely berserk and hit through the clubs. He hit the ball with the 9, 8, 7, 6, 5, 4, 3, 2 and driver. He finally extricated the ball with a shanked 2-wood, chipped on and three-putted for a 19. He called it an "X."

Wilmarth was next. He came down with an acute case of shankitis on 15, which resulted in a quadruple bogey, another quad, a quint, and a final quad. Wilmarth ultimately made the green on each of these holes by kicking the ball with one of his faded white Etonics. Reber considered a comment on the legality of this technique, but was perceptive enough to note the dark red flush on Wilmarth's face.

Reber stayed alive until the last two holes when a spasm of gigantic out-of-bounds-and-gone slices destroyed him. The final blast on 18 cleared a grove of trees and quite possibly caused a distant crashing of glass, what sounded like a low scream and, a few minutes later, several sirens.

And so the sands ran out one more time. The three figures, beaten again, wearily dragged their carts back to the clubhouse. They were mute now, profanitied out. They bought bad coffee from a machine and sat around a table looking straight ahead as the golf dreams receded into the background and the job, the bills, the family, the waistline and the bald spot re-assumed their rightful positions. Reber finally broke the silence.

"Man, I had a 79 wrapped. Fuckleheimer."

Wilmarth was the winner, but shanking had raped him out of a near-perfect round. He bared his fangs at Reber.

"Why don't you learn another word than 'Fuckleheimer'? It's boring. And so is your costume. You look like a sergeant in the Polish army."

Reber blinked, looked down, thought for a long moment, then spoke.

"What's *really* boring, Wilmarth, is your cheating. You cheat so much you must be aware of it. Bernardi and I don't think you could break 100 playing honest."

Wilmarth was furious. He turned to Bernardi.

"Is that right, Bernardi?"

"That's right," said Bernardi.

"Well, as long as we're clearing the air," said Wilmarth, "let's talk about your choice of trophies. They were funny at first; now they're just dumb. Not a riot, not a panic, just dumb."

"I've got to go along with Wilmarth," said Reber. "They're stupid, not funny."

Bernardi looked at the two golfers and smiled sadly, shaking his head.

"How would you guys know what's funny, Reber? The only humor you ever come up with is butchered rehashes of 'I Love Lucy.' I've got to admit, though, that Wilmarth must get a smile from watching people almost faint from his breath."

"Yeah," said Reber, "once in the morning might do it for some people, Wilmarth, but in your case I would suggest twice all day."

Wilmarth stood up and indicated the big gold bowling trophy.

"Did I win that?"

"Yes," said Bernardi, "by cheating."

Much as he wanted the trophy, Wilmarth made the grand gesture.

"Well, you guys can take turns sticking it."

Wilmarth, the martyr, stamped from the coffee shop and slammed the door.

Reber stood up, smiled and shook hands with Bernardi.

"I just made a big decision. I don't want to play golf with you turkeys anymore. I'm socially inept, I dress funny and I'm a klutz. I can't keep up with all the wise talk, and I don't care to try."

"Wait a minute, Reeb," said Bernardi, holding up both hands.

"Hear me out," said Reber. "I've really learned to hate that cheating Wilmarth and his foul breath. But there's something about you that's worse. There's something evil about you, something monstrous, snide and lacerating. The whole trophy thing is a joke to you. I've watched you pretend to congratulate me or Wilmarth when we won. You were always the winner, especially when it was one of your insulting trophies. You are a satanic person and I don't want to have anything more to do with you."

"It's not me," said Bernardi. "Don't you understand, Reeb? It's golf. It's the accursed game. I shank, I kill snakes, I top. I lose brand new balls after one hit and I've been doing things like that for more than 30 years. Things that cause divorces, ulcers, heart attacks and murders. I never once put it all together because I haven't got the ability. But I'm going to luck out some day. And until I do, throwing ice picks and hatchets at you guys keeps me 40 percent sane out there. Should I spend every back nine just crying?"

The tragedy of it all brought tears to Bernardi's eyes. He held up both palms.

"The trophies? Fastest Girl, Best Terrier, or a big schlocky golden bowling ball are exactly what our shanks and slices deserve. Well, what do you think, Reber? Am I sick?"

Reber shook his head and sat down. "No," he said, "not as sick as I am. And I know you know that my stupid little speech was caused by The Great Game, too."

"I know," said Bernardi. "I know."

The door burst open. It was Wilmarth grinning like a cat.

"I came back for my trophy," he said. "And to tell you creeps that I just cured my shank out on the practice tee, so look out."

"Quarter to five next Saturday?" said Reber.

"Quarter to five," said Bernardi.

"Quarter to five," said Wilmarth.

GOLF IS A GAME OF MADNESS

The lunacy of golf is a madness of mud, sweat, rain and darkness. It's an insanity of blisters and bursitis, a quest for pneumonia, sunstroke and lightning. A condition of hopeless hope. A virulent disease as incurable as it is chronic. And it all hinges on the rare but recurring moments of miracle shots—the kind that any hacker can make if he tries often and hard enough.

A scratch golfer, a pro golfer, even a superstar could spend an entire, unsuccessful week trying to pull off such a shot. This is the core motivation of golf, the grand delusion no golfer ever admits to. The obsession that he is not the hacker his score indicates, but something much better. And the recurring moments of miracle prove the lie again and again.

"Wow! Is there a pro alive that could knock in a 56-footer any better than that?"

"Yowee! An inch from the pin from 200 yards out. Could Arnie or Jack do any better?"

If the hacker is big and strong, he'll pull off a miracle drive maybe once every round. He crows as he paces it off: "326, 327, 328 yards! Could the Golden Bear hit a better blast on this hole?"

The answer to all these questions is "No." Thus, the ability to hit pro-level shots is acknowledged, and the matter of consistency is pursued. Surely that big day, when the miracles have all been strung together, is just around the corner. "Let's face it, I've birdied every hole on this course. What's that add up to? 52!" Besides, every golfer knows that three-putt greens and out-of-bounds shots are not his fault. They are the work of some evil spirit.

Hitting a ball with a stick is a malady that only gets worse over the years. And the victim, simultaneously, becomes more and more involved with Mother Nature. At first, the weather is simply there. The fact that it drizzles on Saturday mornings is, after awhile, accepted. But then comes a realization that the weather can in no way become a barrier between the golfer and his golf.

Picnics, garden parties, croquet matches and baseball games can be ruined by bad weather. Golf goes on. The ground can be frozen iron-hard or reduced to gibbering mud. The golfer can be sick, or tired, or depressed, or injured. It doesn't matter. He has a compulsion to get out there and freeze or sweat, wallow in the mud, get soaked or broiled. He'll play anytime of day, before dawn or after dark, and he'll travel great distances to do it.

Rage on the golf course is part of the scene, and it is a fascinating phenomenon. First, because the golfer has such strong motivation to indulge in it; and second, because of the many ways in which he expresses it.

Contact sports, particularly hockey, can drive the participant to violence. The most level-headed man will occasionally crack after prolonged physical abuse accompanied by taunts, jeers and epithets.

But golf, serene golf, has no contact, no taunts, no jeers and no epithets. The brutalizing factor in golf is the constant reminder by the golfer himself of how insufficient, unskilled and unlucky he is.

A golfer who shoots 110 will always have his three dream shots—his unwitting reasons for continuing in the big charade. He will have around 40 "okay" shots; bounding 185-yard drives, half-topped approach shots that make the edge of the green, one and two-foot putts that go in. That leaves 67 rotten shots; these are inexplicably horrible shots that hit trees, land in traps, and plunk down in ponds and creeks; putts that stop nine feet short or eleven feet long; drives that send $1.35 golf balls flying out-of-bounds into deep thickets, never to be seen again. With all of these indignities to contend with, the golfer has a right to express himself from time to time, as the following episodes show.

Situation: A quarter-a-hole match with perennial arch rival. Four straight carry-overs. Par-5 hole. You hit a fantastic 260-yard drive right down the pike that ends up six feet in front of a babbling brook. You decide to gun for the green, to go for a birdie. Maybe an eagle, a double eagle. You top the ball six feet into the babbling brook. You take out a new ball and drop. Now you really have to gun for the green or you are going to lose all that money. What do you do? You again top the ball six feet into the babbling brook.

Solution: Break the club and throw it into the babbling brook.

Situation: It is the last hole of a match. The hole has woods on each side. Your opponent has split the center with his drive. You have smothered one into the left-hand trees. As you line up the ball your alternatives are clear: ignore the fact that your route to the green is completely blocked by a mass of trunks and limbs and just swing away. (This is a gambit developed by a pickle broker named Donald Brown, who once theorized that the area in which tree branches exist is 90 percent air.) Or hit a hook-slice: hook the ball around the first two trees and slice it around the last three. Or take your putter and just rap the ball diagonally to the right into the fairway.

Your opponent, who is watching closely lest you accidentally kick the ball, sports a half-smile. You decide to play safe and then work on him. Remind him of something that upsets and angers him.

On your backswing the putter grazes a branch and thereby deviates your downswing just a tad. You punch the ball and it bounds 20 feet, leaps directly into the center of the trunk of a shagbark hickory and then lazily returns to the precise spot from which you struck it.

Solution: Quickly turn and bang the ball deeper into the woods. Then run over and bash the putter to pieces on the shagbark hickory.

Situation: This supposedly happened at a club in Glencoe, Ill. It was the final hole of the Class C Club Championship. The score was tied. It was a water hole 135 yards long; the green was nestled under the clubhouse veranda. Because of the excitement of the championship in various classes, almost the total membership was in attendance, sipping Bloody Marys and gin and tonics.

Our hero stepped to the tee, lined up—and hit the ball into the water. He proceeded to hit eight more balls, one by one, into the water.

Solution: He unzipped a large compartment in his golf bag, brought forth a dozen new balls and threw them, in threes, all into the water. Then he sailed his furled, red and yellow umbrella into the pond. Next went the clubs, bag and all. He sat down, removed his two-tone golf shoes and heaved them in. In his stocking feet, he walked to the edge of the pond and sailed his fancy golf hat like it was a frisbee.

By this time the blabbering membership had been reduced to silence. Our hero shucked off his alligator shirt and threw that in. He removed his red, white and blue golf slacks, revolved them around in the air like a lasso and let them fly. He finally turned to his shocked opponent, smiled, saluted and leaped into the pond. He swam across, clambered up the opposite bank, and dressed only in a golf glove, socks and a pair of baggy, wet, transparent skivvies, walked majestically through the crowd into the locker room. He never played golf again.

Situation: This supposedly happened at a club near Piedmont, Calif. Our hero was a 40-year-old ex-linebacker with slit-eyes, a bullet head, no neck and a history of violence. It was the 15th hole of a heavy dollar match. Our man was suffering from a severe case of shankitis. He had shanked away many bucks and most of the veneer that distinguishes man from beast. Nobody in the foursome had been crazy enough to even look at him for more than an hour.

On the 15th tee he somehow had managed to shank his drive. It sailed diagonally to the right over the top of the refreshment house and ended up two fairways away. In a murderous calm, he strolled to his ball and was lining up the next shot when a drive missed his left ear by a quarter of an inch. He turned and was greeted from the tee in question with unkind comments from a foursome of college boys.

"Stay in your own fairway, pops."

"Are you lost, old man?"

"Somebody give gramps a map."

"Let's return the old hacker to the home."

Solution: With a primeval scream our hero attacked the college boys, punched hard and shredded off handfuls of sweater. At one time or another, he decked all four. His foursome galloped over to assist and found that it was the college boys who needed help. Two other foursomes arrived, and all parties got involved in subduing the deranged golfer. The lady in the refreshment house called the police and within minutes they arrived, careening over the fairways with mars lights flashing.

Our hero gained a measure of fame that day. He is probably the only golfer ever to leave a golf course face down on the floor of a squad car, wearing one shoe, one pant leg, a bloody smile and a straitjacket.

The whole insane spectacle does have a reward for the inmate. A kind of bent kismet. The golfer knows and expects that a series of disasters will occur. This is the "I-knew-it" philosophical position, usually accompanied by a shrug testifying to the fact that the catastrophe was preordained and had nothing to do with lack of skill. This attitude covers the striking of guy-wires, two-inch trees, one-inch branches and tiny pebbles on greens. By mixing total berserkness with I-knew-it-ism, the golfer is able to retain a measure of sanity—until he is pushed too far.

At this point, as if directed by some diabolical Cecil B. DeMille, a miracle shot is cued in. The golfer is thereby effectively tranquilized until the next brink.

The final and most cynical chapter of The Madness always manifests itself on the 18th hole. It is here that the lunatic is presented with a free-for-nothing miracle shot known to those who understand it as a "comebacker." This chip-in, sunk-blast, or whatever is like pouring honey on the golfer's brain. As he heads for a beer he is too loud and too jovial to hear the ten-thousand-voice celestial choir singing "SUCKER-R-R-R!" in six-part harmony.

THE GOLF GOD

When the pro golf tour hits Royalty Banks Island each spring, the whole place goes bananas. Like the Crosby, celebrities come from all over the country to play in it. And the tycoons come, too. An invite to the RB is a status symbol money can't buy.

For a solid week it's one big golfing houseparty, with the guests and their wives staying at private homes all over the island. The status order on guests is surely defined: celebs first, old pros second, young hot-shots third, tycoons fourth. Any combination gets you more.

The morning after the pro-am banquet I woke up around 6:00 with my head coming off and the room going around. I hadn't been that hung over since VJ Day on Okinawa. I got up, built a pot of coffee and a large Bloody Mary with plenty of Tabasco. I decided to wander over to the club and watch the early starters tee off in the pro tournament.

The clubhouse is 1920's Spanish Colonial, the interior a monument to Dorothy Draper. I walked upstairs to the deck overlooking the first tee and as I sat down on a big striped deck chair, I spilled my coffee all over my right knee.

"On the tee, Eddie Joslyn," said the loudspeaker.

I leaned over to get a closer look. No question, it was a fellow who had worked for me at one time, a crackerjack young lawyer. We had played golf together in company tournaments. He was good in that league. Shot about the way I did, low 80's. But how could he be a professional? He looked ill, skin and bones, with his chin and cheekbones jutting. He was dressed in white with a Ben-Hogan-type cap pulled down almost over his eyes.

He teed up, addressed, and then went into motion with that impossible lazy swing Boros, Littler and others employ. The ball exploded off the club, following the curve of the dogleg and soared far over the big fairway trap I couldn't reach with a howitzer. He turned and nodded his head at the sprinkling of applause.

"Eddie!" I called.

He looked up, smiled and motioned me down.

"Ben! Come on along."

He was glad to see me, almost pathetically so. He put his arm around my shoulder as we walked down the first fairway after the other golfers and the caddies. He was eager to know any news of his cronies at the law firm. His sunken eyes hung on every word.

Eddie's approach shot was about 160 into a small elevated green guarded by two deep traps. He selected a 7-iron, and with no more effort than tossing a card into a hat, hit a towering shot over everything that landed six feet from the hole and backspun to the front fringe. He winced in pain, then quickly smiled.

"Are you okay, Eddie?" I asked.

The other two golfers were looking at him, dead pan.

"Sure, Ben."

He cupped his hand to the side of his mouth.

"Meet me at the practice tee just before dark. I have to talk to you."

I nodded. Something was terribly wrong, and I had to find out what.

Eddie got shaky pars on the first two holes and drove long to the left rough on No. 3. I waved goodbye, nodded and pointed at my watch, stumbled over to my house just off the fairway and slept most of the day.

I woke up cured. Ready to start the booze cycle all over again. Our guests were Hal Dawson and his wife Carrie. We were due at a dinner party down the road with a lot of movie people. I told Annabelle and the Dawsons to go ahead, I'd meet them there.

I took a shortcut through the woods and as I got near the tee I heard wild, whooping rebel yells and loud cackling laughter. The big, blond Titleholder's champion, carrying a couple of woods, came toward me along the path just as another wild yell came from the tee. He shrugged and made the circular "crazy" sign with his finger. I could see Eddie Joslyn was alone on the tee.

"Eddie! What did you shoot today?"

He turned and raised his arms in pathetic gratitude.

"Ben! You showed up. I didn't think you would. Come over here. I have to show you something."

He teed up and with a motion like brushing a few crumbs off a table, poled the ball in a rising line drive about 280 yards dead center. He teed up another ball and extended the club to me.

"Now you hit one," he said.

"Come on, Eddie," I said, "why torment an old man?"

"I just want to make a point, Ben. Imitate my swing."

I took the club and flexed it. My mind raced back 40 years. I was crazy for golf and I had the same illusions every young golfer has after breaking 80 a few times. I'll turn pro, join the tour, play golf every day and get paid for it, maybe win the National Open or the Masters. After walking a tournament or seeing one on the tube, I'd engrave in my brain that impossibly effortless swing the pros have, and race out to try it. It never worked, so I'd give it up and go back to my overswing, speed faster than the naked eye can perceive, and both feet off the ground at impact.

"Swing the same way I did, Ben, please."

I swung and hit a little poop shot, a little pitch and run.

Eddie took the driver back, teed up, imitated my swing and hit a blast well over 300 yards.

"I surrender," I said, "and you're not doing my ego any good."

"Ben," said Eddie, "we both took the same swing at the ball. Mine went down the pike, yours didn't go anywhere. Why?"

"Oh! Just a couple of reasons, like coordination, timing, weight transfer, fingers, wrists, arms, shoulders, hips and legs all interacting like a series of levers, generating tremendous power. Things like that."

Eddie burst out in a wild cackle.

"Ben, Ben, Ben, you've read everything from Hagen to Hogan to Palmer to Miller. All the incredible theories on how to hit a golf ball. And it's all good, up to a point. But no instruction in the world can give you that nothing swing with the big yardage."

"Then where does it come from?"

"The Golf God."

"The Golf God?"

"That's what the guys call him. He gives you the swing."

"He didn't give me the swing."

"Ben, there are two main prerequisites. You have to be pretty good. Better than *you* ever were. And you have to be totally committed to the game. Fifty-four holes a day without lunch. Putting long after dark. Shining the clubs with steel wool in the evenings. Cleaning and polishing your golf shoes. Playing in the rain, the snow and the cold. And you have to hunger, salivate to be a pro. With your hands clenched you pray to be a pro. Now, Ben, don't look at me like that. I know it sounds crazy, but I'm telling you how it works."

"Eddie, does the Golf God then appear along with a clap of thunder?"

"No, it's very simple. You are out on the course, alone, and you are beseeching in your mind to be a pro. Everything gets very quiet, birds stop singing, the wind drops so the trees and bushes are motionless. It's like the whole world stopped. No cars on the road, no lawnmowers on the course. No other golfers in sight. Then he talks. 'Hit the ball,' he says. So you hit with your high-speed swing and you get a better shot than you've ever had. 'Swing slower,' he says. So you drop another ball and take a slower cut at it. And it sort of magically leaps off the club, way longer than you've ever seen except from the pros. 'Slower,' says the Golf God. So you finally get it down to the little easy sweep that knocks the ball out of sight. Booms out so far and so high that galleries just shake their heads in admiration."

Eddie recited all this casually and matter-of-factly. I found myself edging backwards.

"Eddie," I said, "how does the Golf God sound?"

Eddie smiled and shrugged.

"Ben, I know what you're thinking. But I'm telling it

like it is. What's his voice like? I only heard him that one time, but I'd say he's a cross between Charlton Heston and Walter Cronkite. A big voice, authoritative. Like we used to say about certain judges, ballzy."

It was getting dark and I was late for the dinner party. But I couldn't leave.

"Okay, Eddie, so the Golf God gives you the big hit. That's it? No dues to pay?"

Eddie nodded ruefully.

"You pay heavy dues. The Golf God is not bloodthirsty like, say, a Mayan or Incan deity, but he likes to degrade. When I graduated from pro school, a really old pro was apparently assigned to me. He told me what I had to do, over pancakes one morning in a Florida hotel coffee shop. I couldn't believe it. I thought he was putting me on.

"He said that before and during a tournament, all the pros and the chosen amateurs must pay respects, as he put it, to the course. This included: kissing every flagstick, eating a little sand out of every trap, walking on each green on bare knees, spitting on every out-of-bounds marker, chewing and spitting out rough, throwing a new ball into each water hazard."

"Eddie, do you mean to tell me the big pros are in this conspiracy?"

"All of them."

"And they all do those things?"

"Ben, on the days before a tournament it's like Grand Central Station out on the course between midnight and 3 a.m. Hell, last night I saw the National Open champion sitting yogi-style in the big trap in front of the 17th green, eating sand."

"You're kidding."

"You know the slimy lagoon that runs along two-thirds of No. 8? Titleists were splashing in there like hailstones. And some of the boys were actually swimming in that slop. I guess that gives you extra points."

"Why would the Golf God give points for self-degradation?"

"Ah, Ben, there's good logic behind it. These devices,

these acts force the children to know the course. Do I *know* about that big trap behind the 6th green? I wallowed in it and ate part of it. Am I *aware* of the canal on the left side of 14? I swam in it and drank part of it. It's like the joke about the guy training the mule. He hits it over the head with a club, and explains that the first thing is to get the mule's attention. The Golf God is like a third-grade teacher. Kindly, but a total autocrat: 'Don't think, just do as I say'."

Eddie kept teeing and hitting as he talked. It was probably an illusion caused by the lengthening shadows, but both the swing and the ball action seemed to get progressively slower until both appeared to be, literally, slow motion.

"Eddie, why are you talking about it, blowing the whistle? Why don't you just relax and enjoy the life and the money and the publicity?"

Eddie put the club down. "No reflection, Ben, because you're a good guy, always played it straight with me, but pro golf is a lot like the legal business. It's fake. These guys can't really hit the ball. They're a bunch of phonies like the deep-voiced, Brooksie types on Lasalle Street. Golf pros look the part, too. But they're not for real either. I couldn't play the law game anymore, and I'm about out of gas on this one."

"Let me ask you this, Eddie. Why don't all golf pros shoot about the same? I mean, if the Golf God has them do all these weird things, why don't they all get equal treatment?"

"You don't know for sure. The Golf God is a little flaky. A guy can go through an elaborate night-time ceremony and fire a 77 the next day. Or he can perfunctorily kiss a couple of flags, eat a few grains of sand, and go out and shoot a 64. The Golf God maybe liked the fact that he had eggs for breakfast *before* corn flakes, while reading a comic book. Or the Golf God flipped out over the guy petting a cat or hollering at a real estate man or wearing socks that don't match."

"This is getting pretty ridiculous, Eddie."

"Look, the average guy on the circuit has had maybe two or three holes-in-one. Right? Yet *one* guy has made more than 50! And he's nowhere near the best short-iron shot around. And then, look at the guys who've won a really big championship — and then never won another thing! You've got to admit, those circumstances don't leave much room for chance."

"That's all there is to it? You stumble onto something that makes the Golf God happy, and you just rake in the money?"

"Maybe. Or, maybe it's just the idea of trying so hard to please. Whatever it is, I reject it and it's surely killing me. You said I looked bad. I don't weigh over 130 pounds and I have headaches and dizzy spells more and more."

"And I don't imagine you're too popular with the other pros."

"Yeah," said Eddie. "They're giving me the silent treatment, but they're not exactly my type anyway. A jock is a jock. The quintessential thing in most sports is to engineer a ball somewhere. Hardly something to devote your life to. The other pros know I'm shooting my mouth off, but they know I sound crazy. And they know the Golf God will handle it. I figure he'll kill me with lightning. Isn't that the easiest, most logical way to do it? I won't even go near a golf course if it's raining."

"Eddie, I know a good psychiatrist in Atlanta, a fellow I went to school with. I think he could help."

Eddie stared at me with those big sunken eyes and shook his head, sadly.

"You don't believe me, and I don't blame you."

"Eddie, I want to believe you, but look, suppose everybody in a tournament comes up with a pattern that works? Say, a combination of eating sand and wearing socks that don't match. Who wins? And why?"

Eddie smiled and propelled a ball far down the darkening corridor between the trees with a soft, whispery swing that wouldn't have broken a lightbulb.

"That's the really cruel part. The Golf God gives you the swing, the big impossible hit, but he doesn't give you the rest of it: the accuracy, the touch, the precision, unless you're able to concentrate, totally, on even the most routine shots. I'm not.

"Like when I was writing briefs for you guys. They were good and they won me a lot of points because they were inspirational and impulsive, written with about 1/3 of the brain. I'm sure they're dull again, over-thought, weighed-down with heavy hands.

"The Golf God, in all his wisdom, goes the overthink route. When I won the Remberton Classic, up in Oregon, I don't even remember the last two holes. I needed a birdie and an eagle to win, and I got them. But the Golf God made me concentrate so hard I damn near had a brain hemorrhage. I actually passed out in the scoring tent.

"When I'm up to hit, I think about the possibilities and what has to be done, but I think about everything else, too. The weather, what the Knicks did last night, my wife and the kids, the market, what kind of hawk is sailing in the sky. My mind teems with thoughts. And if I can't choke them off, I'm going to hit a gorgeous, soaring blast out-of-bounds. That's the penalty from His Majesty."

"What's the point of the penalty, Eddie?"

"The Golf God doesn't understand about people's minds. He sounds kind, but he's more like Cotton Mather than Walter Cronkite. I have a Phi Beta Key. I think a lot. There are still high school drop-outs on the circuit. And most of the college grads came out of golf colleges which don't exactly feature pre-med, pre-law or Nobel prize winners. I can't stop my mind from thinking and analyzing everything that comes along. The bulk of the guys can. They can be a cow thinking about grass. The concentration required to hit a ball near the pin is about as painful to most of the boys as a tap on the shoulder. To me, it's like a migraine. But again, there's logic in it.

"The Golf God wants his children to tend to business, to stop skylarking, to stop counting their money, or worrying about their wardrobe for the Johnny Carson Show. The concentration pain is like a spanking, designed to hone the mind, underline the seriousness of the shot. Total concentration, which is not only painful but dangerous, can be achieved rarely and only briefly, and results in the impossible shot: the 90-foot putt, the hole-in-one. It's painful even to the average tour jockey. To me it's impossible.

"It's like you're discussing Laurel and Hardy and having a beer. When it's time to pick up the glass and take a sip, concentrate on the whole mechanics of the situation. Open the hand, twine the fingers around the glass, lift the glass, do not tilt or the liquid will spill, raise the glass to the lips, incline your head, tip the glass, et cetera. With the Golf God, nothing is automatic. Like I said, I know why he does it, and I guess it's for the common good."

It was beginning to get dark. The coachlights in front of the houses along the fairways were on. Eddie hit three more impossibly long arching blasts. The balls holding, holding, holding against the red sky. He let out a war whoop after each shot. I wanted to leave, but I couldn't.

"Appeal, Eddie," I said. "Talk to the Golf God. There must be others like you who have a mind."

"There were," said Eddie, "but Johnny Lake is now practicing law in New Jersey. Harry Willkie is in the lumber business. The other two, Clements and Adrito, are in pro golf administration. None of them play competitive golf anymore. Appeal? I've tried. Just a month ago, in Texas, I decided to give it one more big shot. I went out on the course before dawn and picked out the green the first rays of the sun would hit most prominently. I stripped naked and spreadeagled. When the sun peeked over the hills, I yelled, 'Golf God! Golf God!' I heard something, opened my eyes, and looked into the faces of a group of birdwatchers. I ran in one direction and they ran in the other."

Eddie cackled wildly and beckoned me with his finger. I moved closer.

"Ben, I know people are waiting for you. Just one more thing. See those two jackpines on the right edge of the fairway? About 50 yards over there?"

"I see them."

"Okay, watch."

He teed up and hit a low iron that bounced off the right-hand tree into the left-hand tree, then bounced off the left-hand tree and arched back into his outstretched hand. His face was pinched with pain as he handed me the ball.

"Fluke," I said.

He teed up again and repeated the shot precisely. He handed me the second ball. Tears rolled down his cheeks and his teeth were gritted in pain. He turned and walked off into the dark.

I'll admit that to see for myself I did go out on the course the night before the last day of the tournament. I went out at 2 a.m. on the nose, and of course I never saw a soul, either in the traps, the water hazards or on the greens. I felt like an idiot.

I suppose it's possible that at that stage in the tournament with only a small percentage of the players in contention, they paid their respects to the Golf God earlier in the evening. It's also possible that they simply moved out of the way and ducked behind trees or into bushes when I came tripping and cursing along.

I really think poor Eddie Joslyn was nuts, broken down mentally. I think his ricochet shots on the practice tee were flukes. But I'll tell you something that bothers me. About six months after the RB, the pro tour moved into Pensacola. During a qualifying round, a golfer on the first tee apparently lost his concentration for a moment and lined a drive off the tee into the putting area. There were 15 golfers there, either putting or just standing around talking. The ball struck Eddie Joslyn in the left temple, killing him instantly.

THE STORY OF PIETER VAN SCHUYLER

Add to the illustrious names of Gargantua, Bushman, and Mme. Toto that of Pieter Van Schuyler and you'll have the gorilla blue-book complete. And while Gargantua and the rest spent their days glowering at humanity through iron bars, Pieter hobnobs with his admirers, plays Canasta, drinks gin and tonic and, in short, does almost everything but talk. And can that ape sock a golf ball!

Sir Cedric Dunsteed, golf editor of the Capetown (S. Africa) *Daily Caper*, reported the details of Pieter Van Schuyler as follows:

"He was a massive creature an inch under six feet but scaling close to five hundred pounds. His face, though brutish by human standards, contained an air of calm dignity with a trace of sadness. The spectators at the annual West Africa driving tournament buzzed with anticipation and, naturally, gave Van Schuyler wide berth.

"He strode to the tee carrying his own clubs, which I noticed were made by a Cincinnati concern, and with his right foot unzipped the bag and extracted a ball which he flipped into his left hand. He held it high for all to see and then, while whistling some tune I did not know, he crushed it as if it were a grape. I suppose it was cut or damaged in some way. Extracting another he examined it and then tossed it high into the air catching it in his left foot. He placed the ball on the ground (I understand that he never uses a tee) and drew his driver from the genuine alligator bag.

"Far out on the course the man marking the drives held up a large white card reading '325 meters' which was the leading distance thus far, and attained by Cyrus Watkins, famed Egyptian long-ball hitter. Van Schuyler grasped the club in orthodox fashion and went into his backswing. At the top of the swing he froze and held poised for at least a full minute while the gallery held its breath. Then, with a shrill whistle, he smote.

"The ball went for the man with the marker like a tack for a magnet. It started low and stayed low and if the man hadn't flung himself flat, he would have been beheaded. The ball finally came down, took three skidding bounces and stopped. Another man with another marker stepped out from behind a huge mahogany tree and held up his sign—'450 meters.' The gallery roared its approval.

"Peter Van Schuyler, all the while, had remained in follow-through position. Presently a gnome-like little man detached himself from the crowd. He was Johann Van Schuyler, Pieter's foster father and namesake. He had with him a glass of what looked to be un-iced gin and tonic. Pieter turned and threw him a salute. Johann returned the salute, approached, and whispered into a cavernous ear while proffering the drink. Pieter's face wreathed into a grin and he sat down yogi style. Out of the corner of my eye I could see Watkins, the Egyptian, protesting to adamant officials."

Pieter Van Schuyler was found abandoned in the Loch Lomond region of Africa's boundless *veldt* by Johann Van Schuyler, a retired Boer War veteran, who was out riding circuit on his vast peanut plantation.

Johann, known to his neighbors as a cranky old cuss, was strangely touched by the mournful whistling of the lost waif, and took him to his *kraal* near Zambesi. The inherent cleverness of the young ape was soon perceived. He was a perfect mimic. He ate at the table with finesse, excelled at cards after watching the local sharks, and several times was caught smoking a pipe and trying to shave. As an outlet for him old Johann thought of golf.

Pieter learned golf in two minutes on the practice tee— all the golf he was ever to learn, that is. It consisted simply of bashing the ball over 400 yards every time he hit it. His teacher, a young pro named Bobbie Latch, enraptured with the results of the first lesson, played 18 holes with his amazing protege—a round which proved to be the only one that Pieter ever played. For it was found that the ape had absolutely no depth perception. On a nice, short 135-

yard, par-3 hole — bang — he would hit one 400 yards straight down the middle! On an easy pitch shot after one of his drives—bang—400 yards over the green!

Victor Von Sphincter, famed Viennese oculist, explained this phenomenon saying that the gorilla's eyes have pupils that are distended and convex, thus destroying automatically any trace of depth perception. Asked if glasses could correct this innate defect, Von Sphincter replied in the affirmative but stated that such glass would require a prismic combination some 17 inches in length, which would make it possible for Pieter to perceive distance but would probably prevent him from seeing the ball in front of him.

Pieter Van Schuyler was thus forced by nature to limit his golfing prowess to driving tournaments. And although he was the best in the world, he had to retire from competition at an early age.

It seems that Pieter's mentor and namesake was also quite a swinger. He was, in fact, known as the "Tanganyika Tangler." Young Pieter was witness to several amorous episodes and, upon reaching adolescence, aped them with violent romantic overtures to officials and competitors at various driving competitions. On more than one occasion it took a tranquilizer gun to subdue him. The end of his golf career finally came the day he vaulted into the judge's box, picked up the governor of Bakuba and gave him a kiss.

Back home in the jungle Pieter met a young lady gorilla named Gwen. She and Pieter eventually had a youngster, named Ruben, who has become quite a tennis player. The young fellow hits green mangoes with plenty of topspin and seems to be developing an awesome two-handed forehand.

THE GOLFER

The police were having great difficulty controlling the crowd, so more police had been summoned and were beginning to arrive. The tires of the wheeling squad cars and motorcycles kicked gravel from the driveway onto the well-fed lawns and immaculate flower beds. The roar of the engines and screams of the sirens were multiplied as they echoed off the ramparts of the venerable Tudor-revival clubhouse. It was an orderly crowd but so vast in size that each small surge snapped ropes, knocked down signs and took out clumps of rhododendron. More than 127,000 people were on hand at the Portmanteau Country Club to greet the greatest golfer the world had ever known—Harold Ribbon—who was about to tee off in quest of his fourth straight National Open title.

No other golfer—not Bobby Jones, Walter Hagen, Nelson, Hogan, Snead, Nicklaus or Palmer—had ever come close to the golfing record of Harold Ribbon. Since his debut at the Masters three years before, Ribbon had won every tournament he entered, 134 straight victories. In his one year as an amateur he eclipsed Jones' immortal Grand Slam by winning the amateurs and opens of 12 countries in addition to those of Britain and the United States. And as a professional Ribbon had wiped out every existing PGA record. His competitive round of 49 will likely stand forever. It was scored at Pebble Beach and was made up of 15 birdies, two eagles and an amazing triple-eagle—an ace on a dogleg par-5.

But it wasn't Harold Ribbon's incredible golfing skills and his flawless swing alone that commanded such huge crowds and such adoration. It was his hacker's heart. He never seemed to believe the shots he hit. He acted as amazed and incredulous as the galleries. His anxiety over a difficult shot seemed as genuine as his amazement at pulling it off. He would clap his forehead and fall flat on his back in a mock faint after holing a twisting 35-footer. He would shake his head in amazement and shrug magnificently to the gallery after slamming a 1-iron stony from 250 yards out. And whereas most professional athletes move with an easy, casual grace, Harold was all jerks, jangles and bumbles. He walked splay-footed and off-balance. He sometimes tripped over his own feet.

But that magnificent golf swing made up for everything. It was often compared to Ace Perkins' picture-book swing. The address, the backswing, the follow-through and the finish were all Perkins. But the comparison ended there. The ball-action was entirely different. Perkins would hit the ball with a classic click-sound and the ball would soar into the air like a giant home run. When Harold Ribbon hit the ball, it seemed almost to explode off the face of the club and would fly outward at terrific speed like a projectile. A good drive for Perkins was 280 yards. On par-5 holes, Ribbon would often hit the ball close to 500 yards. And when he used a more lofted club, he would hit the ball to astonishing altitudes from which it would fall, bounce straight up and die. How Ribbon was able to generate such remarkable power from such unremarkable arms and shoulders was a great mystery.

The quiet mass of people encircling the Portmanteau clubhouse suddenly came to life. A thousand arms pointed to the sky and a mighty cheer went up. High in the clear, cloudless blue they had spotted a red dot that grew steadily larger. It was unmistakably Harold Ribbon's jet-helicopter. It whooshed in, barely clearing a giant oak, and then went into a bank before landing lightly on the clubhouse roof. The crowd began to chant, "Rib-bon! Rib-bon! Rib-bon! Rib-bon!" The copter door opened and a figure dressed in scarlet jumped out and walked lightly to the edge of the roof facing the main body of the crowd. A thundering roar welcomed him and then the chant started again. Ribbon led the chant by swinging his arms like a musical conductor. He was a scrawny young man with an Adam's apple the size of a tangerine. He was dressed in scarlet from hat to shoes, and the large golf cap and billowing plus-fours gave him an old-fashioned look. The huge, black-rimmed glasses he wore were reminiscent of a grammar-school sissy.

Ribbon waved at the crowd for silence, grabbed a bull-horn from the helicopter and said, "Who's a sweet swinger?"

"Rib-bon!" the crowd yelled.

"Who's going to tear this course apart?"

"Rib-bon!" they yelled.

"Who's going to teach Ace and Bull another lesson?"

"Rib-bon!"

Everybody loved Harold's kidding—everybody except a group of five grim-faced men in identical black topcoats and homburgs. They stood off by themselves near the first tee, wincing and gritting their teeth at every cheer. Their leader was sporting-goods tycoon Leroy Dixon, a cruel-looking man in his early 60's. He smiled tightly and gestured at Harold Ribbon in the distance.

"Look at Mr. Popularity! He makes me sick to my stomach."

Dixon pulled out a long black cigar and clipped off the end with a gold cutter. He lighted up leisurely.

"Well, the greatest golfer in the world gets his in exactly 1 hour and 42 minutes."

The men in the black topcoats laughed nastily and elbowed each other in the ribs. Dixon rubbed his hands together in glee. Over at the clubhouse the rooftop show had ended but the crowd was still there, shouting "Rib-bon! Rib-bon! Rib-bon!" A gentle breeze floated in from the west, rustling the leaves of the giant oaks and elms. The brightly dressed people, wearing sunglasses and carrying cardboard periscopes, began to drift toward the first tee. The National Open was about to start.

Harold was somehow aware of the danger in the crowd. From his high perch he saw something, maybe the sun ricocheting off a gun barrel, or a hostile movement in the vast throng. So even as he led his own cheers he casually moved his head from side to side to upset the aim of any sharpshooter. Harold knew that Leroy Dixon and his men were out there somewhere and that they would do anything to keep him from winning his fourth straight National Open title.

Among Harold's many fans clustered around the rooftop door were the governor, senators, the Portmanteau Club president, assorted wives and daughters, the press, a famous comedian and a young lady with a fantastic superstructure draped with a banner reading "Miss National Open." An average turnout, Harold thought. He was charming, courtly. He shook all the hands, kissed the beauty queen, gave six autographs and then ducked into the Portmanteau Club attic. There was just time enough before tee-off to get downstairs for his locker room ritual.

Harold was a physical disaster. He was built like a sick jockey, a starving Arnold Stang. His physique made Woody Allen and Don Knotts look like neighborhood bullies. Any healthy 12-year-old girl could run him off the block. But Harold could hit the ball three tons. Nobody had his power—not Nicklaus, not Palmer, nobody. His compensation for a lack of bodily strength was, apparently, an excess of bodily strength. How it was generated by his milky-white 120 pounds was an endless cause of shrugging puzzlement to the other golfers. And Harold did everything he could to increase the confusion.

The dark-paneled locker room was boiling with activity, but when Harold arrived the shouts and laughter died as soon as they realized he was there. You could almost feel the reverence.

"It's Ribbon."

"Harold's here."

"The champ."

"Hey, Ribbon!"

"Harold, baby!"

Harold nodded judiciously as he walked, occasionally pointing left or right in acknowledgement. When he arrived at his locker area, he noted with satisfaction that everything was ready.

Harold's remarkable wardrobe required an entire bank of lockers, and the effect was like a day-glow rainbow. Some 40-odd ensembles with a long, precise bottom layer of shoes to match. The two lockers on the extreme left were filled with food and equipment—gimmicks that were part of an unending series of hoaxes Harold perpetrated on his fellow professionals, especially the big muscular jocks.

They were all there: wheat germ, barbells, vitamin pills, tonics, a medicine ball, an exercycle, assorted hand and arm exercisers, chocolate bars, electric vibrators and a store of braces and bandages. In each new tournament Harold would "discover" a new way to gain and sustain the great strength he needed to sock his ball so far. At Palm Springs, the week before, Harold had shown the boys what he called "winging." The hands are clasped on top of the head causing the elbows to jut out, winglike. The elbows are then rapidly flapped back and forth.

"If you want to hit a long ball," Harold had said to giant Bull Babson, "you need extra strength in your back. Winging helps me."

As he undressed, Harold noted with satisfaction that several of the pros near him were doing a little winging. For the Open, Harold came up with a new wrinkle. He called it chin-ball. To demonstrate it, Harold wrapped a towel around himself and moved out, tossing a red tennis ball up and down. He looked like a young Gandhi. He moved down the corridor and picked out the biggest, strongest looking kid he could find.

"What's your name, son?"

"Jim Jasper, Mr. Ribbon."

"Call me Harold, Jim. May I give you some sound advice?"

"I would be honored, sir, I mean Harold."

Harold looked suspiciously from side to side.

"Okay, Jim, move in a little closer. No sense telling everybody. Golf is a lot easier if you can move the ball out there. I mean *out* there."

"Yes, sir, I wish I could hit 'em like you do, Mr. Ribbon, Harold."

"You need power in the shoulders, Jim, power in the shoulders," said Harold, flexing a pair that looked like they came from Sweetbriar.

"And, Jim," said Harold, "chin-ball works."

"Chin-ball?" said Jim.

"Shhh!" said Harold. "You take a red tennis ball and you tuck it under your chin."

Harold demonstrated.

"Then grit your teeth, and bob your head up and down as fast as you possibly can."

Harold looked like he was having some kind of spasm. He noticed out of the corners of his eyes that several pros were sneaking a peek.

"All right, Jim, you try it."

Harold tossed him the ball and Jim began bobbing like an idiot.

"Feel it?" said Harold. "Feel it in the shoulders?"

Jim nodded, grinning as he bobbed.

"Chin-ball builds muscle power," Harold assured him.

Harold's amazing career had begun in a big, brooding Victorian mansion in Boston. He had graduated, magna cum laude, from Harvard and M.I.T. and had been snapped up by Orbitronics Industries and stuck into pure research. In an old section of the city, he had an attic apartment overlooking a paved brick street lined with ancient oak trees. His room encompassed the entire attic —a big, crazy room, all angles and eaves. It was furnished basically in Victorian, with a big, brass bedstead, marble-top chest, globe lights and a huge roll-top desk on which sat a double-angle student lamp. Stuffed birds glared from table tops and window sills. Harold's books and scientific equipment were mixed into the scheme. An atomic-weight chart hung on one wall. An old library table in the tower contained test tubes in racks, a centrifuge, a microscope, dials, gauges and miscellaneous scientific glassware. The room was comfortable, kooky, Victorian—and very technical. It was in this room, this attic in Boston, that the great Harold Ribbon learned to play golf.

Harold's position at Orbitronics was ideal. The people he worked with were bright, quick and stimulating. Computer-related project possibilities seemed limitless. Harold felt fulfilled every day, as his mind was pulled and stretched through project problems. At Q-R-7, the research wing, Harold was utilized as a floating consultant, and in a given day he would participate in the fun parts of as many as a dozen problems. Harold couldn't get enough of it. Often, he would get to Orbitronics before dawn and not return to his apartment until after midnight.

But something happened. The zip slowly went out of Harold. He began to oversleep and then get home early. His puny shoulders slumped. He dragged around and began staying in his room on weekends instead of biking to the public gardens or over to Cambridge.

One day Orbitronics called. They were concerned about Harold. He hadn't been at work for three days and they were in quite a bind without him. Harold's landlady, Miss Becknell, checked his room. He wasn't there. That evening she sat on the front steps and waited. Finally, he pedaled in, glowering and talking to himself, parked the bike and pointed at Miss Becknell.

"Get off my back!" he warned.

He marched into the house and on down the hall into the kitchen. She followed him. He turned around and pointed at her again.

"I have a special announcement to make," he said. "It's farewell-cruel-world for this kid. It's the whole jock thing all over again, Miss Becknell. It's a jock world now, before, and for evermore."

"What do you mean, 'It's a jock world,' Harold?"

Harold got up and began to pace.

"It all started when I was about seven years old back on the farm in Bensenville, Ill. We were stealing pumpkins from old man Habermeyer's patch. I saw the pumpkin I wanted. Leonard Mecklenberg wanted the same one. So he beat me up and took it. Leonard Mecklenberg was a seven-year-old mesomorph, a jock. And I was, and am, not only an ectomorph, but a short one, and a totally uncoordinated one—a physical negative."

"Come on, Harold! A person's physical appearance or

ability isn't the whole world," said Miss Becknell.

"Ah, but it is! It's the whole thing. Through grammar school and high school I was chased and beaten by assorted Leonard Mecklenbergs. I don't know how many dozen times I had to climb trees to get my hats or pants because Leonard Mecklenbergs threw them up there. The Leonard Mecklenbergs starred in all the sports. They got all the girls. They won all the top class offices. They got all the good summer jobs. They got everything."

"But, Harold," Miss Bucknell pointed out. "There are other ways of achieving. . . ."

"Compensate!" he shouted. "Sure, compensate! I became the world's champion compensater. I won all the spell-downs. I raised prize chickens. I got straight A's. I made sensational model airplanes. None of it meant a thing. I was still Harold, the weirdo, without girls, cheers or jobs.

"At college, at least there were other weirdos like me. But the jocks still reigned, still had it all. The big difference was I knew my day was coming. There's only one thing American business really cares about—the buck. Let the jocks have all the fun while they can, us weirdos will make the bucks. We'll be the ones that run the show."

"So?"

"So, do you know what I found out last week?" said Harold in a very quiet voice. "I found out that Orbitronics Industries is run by Leonard Mecklenbergs!"

He counted on his fingers.

"The chairman, the president, the six vice presidents and the nine honchos from other companies. Not *one* dwarf, gnome or troll."

"All right, Harold, so that's the way it is. What are you going to do about it?"

What Harold decided to do was become a golfer. He had reasoned that no other sport—with the possible exceptions of riflery, archery or pool—offered the amateur participant an occasional flash of top-level, professional proficiency. Could a myopic, 40-year old with a pot belly and spindly little white legs hit a baseball out of Yankee Stadium, run over a linebacker for a touchdown, or out-rebound an N.B.A. center? Never. Could he sink an approach shot, or a long, twisting, side-hill putt? Sure he could.

The first thing Harold did after making his big decision was to visit a rundown driving range on the outskirts of the city. It was feebly lighted by 60-watt bulbs strung on wires. A hand-painted sign said "Milo's Stop 'n Sock." The proprietor was a short, fat unshaven man in his 50's with a stub of an unlighted cigar stuck between his lips. He looked dubiously at Harold's knickers. Harold grinned.

"I'm Harold Ribbon," he said, extending his hand. "I guess you're closed for the night?"

"Not yet I ain't."

"Well, how much is it to golf?"

"A buck and a half."

Harold handed him some change and received in return a wire basket filled with golf balls with red rings around them, and a golf club. Harold took the basket and the club to one of the tees. He set the basket down, took off his coat and selected a ball. He gripped the club baseball style, threw the ball in the air and hit a pop-fly with the shaft. He picked up another one. He hit two more. Milo leaned out of the shack.

"Hey!" he yelled. "What are you, a wise guy? Hit the ball off the ground, if you don't mind."

Harold put the next ball on the ground and grasped the club with the head upside down. He took a huge, awkward swipe, missed the ball, swung back like a left-hander, and connected with a backwards line drive that almost decapitated the properietor. The ball slammed into the back of the stand with a report like a cherry bomb.

Milo disappeared. As he slowly raised his head to peer out at Harold, another shot came through and slammed into the back of the stand. Milo crouched fearfully out of sight with his hands and arms over his head. He then took out a handkerchief, tied it to a golf club and cautiously raised a flag of truce.

"What's the matter," yelled Harold.

Milo got to his feet with great dignity. He carefully dusted himself off and opened a door in the rear of the stand. He walked slowly up to Harold, stopped and looked at him dead pan. He spoke very calmly.

"I think there's something wrong with the way you swing. It's not smooth."

"Who would you say has a real smooth swing?"

"You mean what golfer has a smooth swing? All them pros do. I guess Ace Perkins is the smoothest."

"Ace Perkins?"

"Ace Perkins. Now look, swing easy and try to hit the ball out toward the signs—not toward the shack. Just take it easy, real easy."

"Okay," said Harold. And from then on he began to learn the fundamentals of the golf swing.

The next day at Orbitronics was Harold's day in the barrel. It was his day in the rotation, to be in charge of the computer room. Most of the young geniuses dreaded this duty, but Harold enjoyed it. It was like a day off, a holiday from the heavy stuff. And Harold had worked out a special routine to handle it.

The computer room at Orbitronics Industries was about the size of a football field. The walls and floor were of pale green tile. The ceiling was about 40 feet high and was one solid, glowing light source. The computers themselves were arranged geometrically on the floor like a maze with frequent cul de sacs. Between the tops of the computers and the ceiling were criss-cross catwalks used for observation and maintenance.

Grasping a clipboard in one hand, Harold stood in front of a control panel and began to push buttons and throw switches. One after the other the banks of computers went into action. Lights flashed off and on in various patterns. Oscilloscopes wiggled and tapes spun. Each computer as it reached operating speed had a characteristic sound. Some buzzed, some clanked, some whistled and some belched.

Harold cocked his head and listened carefully. He raised his pen as if it were a baton and kept time. He leaned from one side to the other and directed as if to the violin section, to the tympani, to the woodwinds and to the brass. He was dressed for the occasion. He wore his navy blue high school graduation coat, white shirt and black knit tie, his Phi Beta Kappa key, a pair of formal gray flannel knickers, high black stockings and gleaming brown and white saddle shoes.

Apparently satisfied with the sound of the computer orchestra, he began a strange dance in perfect time to the rhythm. He twirled and swooped as he went from dial to gauge making notations on the clipboard. He moved from one end of the room to the other doing his bizarre but skillful improvisation of ballet, jitterbug, frug, watusi and Charleston. He bobbed and weaved; he did bumps and grinds; he bunny-hugged and waltzed from machine to machine.

"Harold Ribbon!"

An exasperated, plump gentleman in his 60's appeared suddenly from between two units of the vast complex of machines. He wore a dark, three-piece suit and round, gold-rimmed glasses. He looked like a grammar school principal. He was Harold's boss.

"Yes, sir! Mr. Garley," said Harold, dropping his clipboard.

"Ribbon, I know that you are very efficient. I know that you are very bright. And I know that our little company was very lucky to get you. *But I don't like your dancing!*"

"I'm sorry, Mr. Garley," said Harold.

"And another thing. *I don't like those knickers!* The only people who wear knickers, Ribbon, are golfers. Are you a golfer?"

Garley wheezed and laughed at his joke. Harold looked sadly down at his knickers and fanned them out with his thumb and forefingers.

"I want to be a golfer. I'm just learning. Mr. Garley, do you play golf?"

97

"Yes, Ribbon, as a matter of fact I do."

"Mr. Garley, have you ever heard of Ace Perkins?"

"Have I ever heard of Ace Perkins! Why, he's won more tournaments than any other golfer in history. Ace Perkins is my idol."

"Then he has a smooth swing?"

"A smooth swing? You're darn tootin' he has a smooth swing!"

After work that day, Harold pedaled to a bookstore, a department store, a sporting goods store and a camera shop. At each stop, he added more packages until he looked like an overloaded Mexican burro.

He pedaled zig-zaggingly back to his apartment and dumped everything on the floor. At one end of the room he placed a large framework with a canvas sheet hanging from it. The center of the sheet had a painted bull's-eye. Heavy netting extended out at right angles from the target for 15 to 20 feet. It was a home golf driving range, which Harold completed by setting into position a driving mat with a rubber tee that jutted up. Next, he set up a large moving screen about eight feet square. Behind the screen he positioned a 35-millimeter motion picture projector aimed into prisms mounted on a tripod.

Harold plugged in the projector and turned it on. A life-sized image of Ace Perkins flashed onto the screen. Perkins swung and hit the ball. Harold ran the same film over and over again.

Next, he pulled a large mirror into position opposite the rear-screen projection, so that the Perkins footage was perfectly mirrored between the screen and the mirror. Then he set up the rubber driving mat, selected a club from a carton of new clubs, and placed a ball on the rubber tee. In synchronization with the Ace Perkins image, Harold swung. He was almost totally uncoordinated. His swing was a combination of a push and chop. He hit the ball between the mirror and the netting and it smashed a window. He teed up again and hit a ball diagonally to the left, smashing a large Victorian globe lamp. He teed up again, missed the ball completely, and backhanded it on a line that narrowly avoided a bust of Shakespeare and obliterated the rear window of the room.

After months of almost constant practice—and dozens of broken panes of glass—Harold was dejected. He hit the depths one night in the dead of winter. Snow covered the ground. In front of Harold's apartment house two children were making a snowman. Suddenly three loud crashes were heard in rapid succession and three striped balls fell from the attic window, one ball landing on the snowman's head and the other two narrowly missing the children, who screamed and ran away.

Inside, Harold was in despair as he stood in position at the driving mat between the mirror and the ever-repeating image of Ace Perkins hitting a golf ball.

"I just don't have it," he wailed to Miss Becknell. "I'm through! I don't think I've hit that bull's-eye more than five times in six months. I just don't have the right kind of muscles or coordination or something. I've studied Ace Perkins' swing, memorized every inch of it. My mind knows exactly how to do it. But the message doesn't get through to the arms and wrists and hands."

Harold sat on the floor. He was in real despair. Miss Becknell was quite sympathetic.

"Poor Harold. You've tried so hard. It doesn't seem fair that a brilliant mind like yours can't accomplish everything it wants to. It doesn't seem fair that you can't somehow teach yourself to swing this silly golf club."

Miss Becknell picked the club up and looked at it quizzically. Harold looked up. His eyes and mouth popped open.

"What did you say about teaching?"

"I said it's a shame you can't teach yourself to swing this silly golf club."

"That's it. *Teach!* Miss Becknell, you've given me the answer! I can't teach myself to swing a golf club, but I'll bet I can teach it to swing itself!"

"Oh, Harold! How can you do that?"

"The same way you can teach a garage door to open by itself—with electronics!"

Harold took a week off from Orbitronics and worked day and night on his new idea. The Ace Perkins rear-screen projection was still in operation, but something new had been added. A golf club held by rods and clamps was freely swinging in the same arc as the Ace Perkins golf club, and in perfect synchronization. Harold watched it swing and then touched the handle of the club. It stopped automatically. He unclamped the club, took it over to his driving range, and teed up a striped ball. Then, as he went into the backswing the club began pulling him sideways across the room in an erratic pattern. It was as if the club was alive. Harold was pulled in drunken circles and spun about. He pushed the end of the handle and the twirling stopped.

He tried again and this time the backswing was perfect and he socked the ball real well, but his follow-through dragged him at high speed into the target, collapsing the entire range and shrouding him in canvas and netting. Miss Becknell burst into the room.

"Harold? Are you all right?"

Harold began to extricate himself from the collapsed range.

"Hi! Miss Becknell, I'm fine, but this golf club needs a few minor adjustments."

Harold walked over to his workbench. He clamped the shaft of his driver in a vise so that the head of the club was facing upward. Then he loosened the screws holding the face of the club, removed the face, and lifted out a strange, complicated mechanism. The club had been hollowed out—it was an empty shell.

"You see, the club is run by these little tiny gyroscopes," Harold explained to Miss Becknell. "They're sealed, but they have little wheels inside just like the gyroscopes you used to play with when you were a kid. The kind that balance on a string. The gyroscopes are run by these little transistors—see—right here? When I turn this little battery on, everything starts working. The gyroscopes are set in a pattern—in this case, it's Ace Perkins' swing. Gyroscopes are quite powerful. When they're set a certain way you can't go against the pattern. It does exactly what it's taught to do—and it does something else. See this faceplate?"

Harold pointed at the hitting surface of the mechanism. He reached into his pocket and pulled out a striped golf ball. He put the golf ball on the rubber tee and, bending way over, slowly moved the hand-held mechanism toward it. When the mechanism barely touched the ball there was a click and the ball was propelled into the target as if shot from a gun.

Harold stood up. He held out the mechanism.

"When contact is made with this faceplate, it snaps."

Harold touched the faceplate with a pencil and it clicked authoritatively.

"That'll send a ball 150 yards without even swinging. Now Miss Becknell, sit tight. You're going to see a demonstration."

Harold made one last adjustment before putting the mechanism back inside the hollowed-out clubhead. He teed up a striped ball, swung in perfect imitation of Ace Perkins and rocketed the ball into the target where it smacked like a pistol shot. He teed up again and crashed another perfect shot. Miss Becknell was ecstatic.

"Harold, you've done it! You're going to be the world's greatest golfer!"

And so Harold Ribbon set out to make his fortune.

The nearby village of Wortham, Mass., is often called the golf club capital of the world. In its confines are the major manufacturers of clubs, balls, bags, even tees. The Dixon Sporting Goods Company, largest of them all, covered many square blocks and had great rows of chimneys puffing in perfect unison. The letters in the name "Dixon" were so large that they sprawled across the roof for almost a quarter of a mile. The factory was painted silver and was spotlessly clean.

Harold Ribbon, dressed in full golf garb and carrying his clubs on his back, rode his bike to the administration building and leaned it against the wall. He entered the reception room.

"I'd like to see Mr. Dixon," said Harold to the receptionist.

"Whom shall I say is calling?"

"Harold Ribbon. He doesn't know me. But I have a fantastic invention to show him."

"I see."

She punched an intercom button.

"Mr. Lacey, there's a person out here named Harold Ribbon to see Mr. Dixon. The person is wearing a red cap, yellow sweater and knickers. The person has a bag of golf clubs over his shoulder and the person says he has a quote, fantastic invention, unquote, to show Mr. Dixon. The person doesn't look too b-r-i-t-e."

"Thank you, Miss Joselyn," hummed a baritone executive voice.

Miss Joselyn looked up at Harold and gave him a phony smile.

"Mr. Dixon is very busy. Mr. Dixon's chief assistant is Mr. Lacey. Mr. Lacey will be here in a moment."

Mr. Lacey appeared. He looked unhappily at Harold. Lacey was very Ivy League, very jock and had his blonde hair parted in the center like F. Scott Fitzgerald. He was brusque and unsmiling.

"What's the invention?"

"Well, Mr. Lacey, it's a new kind of golf club. You see . . ."

"A new kind of golf club? Those look like regular golf clubs. Except you've got them painted silly colors. Wait a minute, those were made by us. Our cheapest model."

"Yes," said Harold. "That's why I came here. I've made a major modification in these golf clubs."

Lacey was irritated and impatient.

"Well, what does it *do?* What's the purpose?"

"It makes it possible for anyone who uses these clubs to be a star golfer," said Harold, grinning and gesturing with both arms.

Lacey stared at Harold. Then he glanced at Miss Joselyn and nodded slightly. She pushed a button and a huge man in a plant police uniform rushed into the room and grabbed Harold. He literally picked him up and carried him toward the front door.

Lacey waved to Harold. "Good-bye, Mr. Ribbon!"

After getting the bum's rush out the door, Harold pulled a pencil and notebook out of his pocket and crossed out "Dixon" on his list of Wortham's sporting goods companies.

His next stop was the Johnson Sporting Goods Company. It was not as big as Dixon, but still a large company. He parked the bike, walked up the stairs and in through the doors. In less than a minute the doors opened and Harold came hurtling out, followed by the golf clubs.

It was the same story at Jorgenson Sporting Goods, Ludden Sporting Goods and Cranshaw Sporting Goods. Harold crossed them all off his list. There was only one name left: Apex Sporting Goods.

Harold found Apex only after a long search amid the cornstalks and sycamore trees that grew in profusion 20 miles outside of Wortham. Louis Apex greeted Harold warmly and, after hearing his story, remarked, "Don't say another word. The whole picture is clear. You took the clubs to Dixon, Johnson, Jorgenson, Ludden and 'Melon-head' Cranshaw. And they all threw you out. Well, Ribbon, don't feel badly about coming here last. I'd have done the same thing. Now! These clubs really work?"

"They really work!" said Harold.

"Will you show me?"

Harold grinned. A few minutes later, he and Mr. Apex were on their way to Milo's Stop 'n Sock. As they approached the shack, the fat proprietor leaned out and stared at Harold in fear and astonishment. He reached up in panic, tripped a rope, the shack's front section slammed down over the opening like a drawbridge, and the shack was closed.

Mr. Apex convinced Milo to open the door wide enough to pass through a basket of balls and a driver with red stripes painted on it. They went over to the tee and Harold took his own driver out of his golf bag, teed up a ball and prepared to swing.

"Hold it!" said Apex. "Use this club."

"Use that club! I can't hit the ball with a regular club."

"That's what I want to see."

Harold shrugged, took the club and addressed the ball. He swung and missed three times before finally pulling off his patented backward shot. Missing the ball initially as usual, he caught it backhanded and lined it straight at the golf shack. Milo had the front section open only about a foot but the ball tore through this opening. There was a yell, a crash and the section slammed closed.

"See what I mean?" said Harold.

"I see what you mean," said Apex. "Now with the other club."

Harold teed up another striped ball, addressed it and swung. The swing was perfection—the pure classic, Ace Perkins swing. The ball started out low and then rose, sailed past the 250-yard marker, went over a fence into a pasture and hit a cow on the fanny. Harold then hit a series of perfect golf shots—long soaring drives off a swing that was a pleasure to watch.

"Okay," said Apex. "Okay, my turn."

Apex teed up a ball. He grasped Milo's golf club and and swung suddenly and violently. He had one of those golf swings that is flat in form and spasmodic in operation. He hit a real banana ball, followed by three more that acted about the same.

"All right, Harold, now let me use your club."

"When you're all set in position you simply press the end of the club. That puts the batteries in contact with the transistors that run the gyroscopes. When you finish the shot either press the end of the club again to turn it off, or unwind the shot in the same arc and then turn it off."

"Why do I have to wait till I'm in position?"

"Because the club is built to go in a certain prescribed arc—the arc of Ace Perkins' swing. The moment you activate the gyroscopes the club will move only in the arc. If you are walking and you accidently turn it on it will stop you. If you address the ball off line, you'll have a perfect swing, but you'll miss the ball completely."

"Okay, I got you."

Apex teed up a ball, pressed the end of the club, waggled in his address and swung. The swing was perfect, and so was the shot.

"Wow!" yelled Apex.

He teed up 17 more times and hit 17 more perfect shots, yelling "Wow!" after each one. He finally ran out of golf balls.

"Fantastic!" he said. "Really fantastic! Of course you know that golf clubs like these are illegal."

"Illegal?" said Harold.

"Completely illegal," said Apex. "Rule No. 2, 2b, of the USGA golf rules says: 'No part of the club may be movable or adjustable!'"

Harold couldn't believe it. He shook his head.

"Illegal, but who cares?" Apex continued. "The only place a rule like that would be enforced would be in a tournament. The average Joe doesn't play in tournaments. He gets up at 3:00 Saturday morning, drives 68 miles, hacks around in about 134 strokes and goes home mad. What these clubs are going to do for this guy is miraculous. He can become a giant. All his drives will go 300 yards or more, instead of 175. No more slices, no more dubs. He shoots over the dogleg. He's always gunning for birdies. He's home in two on all the par-5s. He's got pride in his game and the only question is whether he's in the high 60's or the low 70's. He's a man. He goes home happy and kisses his wife and kiddies. Harold-baby, these clubs are going to be the greatest boon to modern man since the power lawn-mower."

Harold felt much better.

"Then you'll manufacture these clubs, Mr. Apex?"

"Well, Harold, I've got a hunch that these clubs are never going to be manufactured by *anybody*."

"What?"

"You hear stories every once in a while about an amazing new carburetor that lets you get 100 miles to a gallon of gas. The thing never gets on the market because the oil companies buy the invention for a few million bucks and stash it away."

"What's that got to do with these clubs?"

"Plenty. It would be to the advantage of the people who run golf—and believe me that includes birds like Dixon— if these clubs never existed."

"I don't see why. You said everybody would want a set."

"Look. Let me get Dixon and the others over here and then you can hear it from their lips. I'll go phone them."

A parade of Cadillacs, Lincolns and Rolls Royces arrived at Milo's Stop 'n Sock. Gravel was kicked in all directions and doors were slammed. The tycoons were angry. Board meetings had been interrupted, domino and card games had been ruined. Two of the men had been in meetings at their brokerages, another had been summoned from his tennis court and was still in whites. The men clustered around a tall man with white hair, a jutting jaw and a cruel mouth. Harold recognized him from pictures in the newspapers as the legendary Leroy Dixon. Harold tapped Apex on the shoulder.

"What did you say to get all these big wheels to come?"

"Oh, nothing. I just hit these babies where they live. I told them they were as good as bankrupt if they didn't get right over here," said Apex.

He grinned and strode toward the group of advancing executives.

"Well, well, well, I see everybody's here. How nice of you gentlemen to come!"

"Knock it off, Apex," said Dixon. "Whatever this is, it had better be good!"

"Okay. Okay! Gents, this is my associate, Mr. Harold Ribbon. He has invented and constructed a new kind of golf club. Harold, would you give us a demonstration?"

Harold teed up and poled a long, soaring shot into the pasture.

"I didn't come out here to see a golfing exhibition!" said one of the executives.

"A little patience, please," said Apex. "Now, it's my turn."

Apex teed up and blasted one out of the park.

"So what?" said Dixon. "You've always been a golfer, Apex."

"Not that kind of a golfer. Anyway, now it's your turn, Leroy. Come here. I'll show you how to use this club."

Dixon grudgingly consented and the rest of the group crowded around. Apex teed a ball and then stepped back.

"Okay, sock away!"

Dixon swung and hit one of those drives that starts out low, begins to rise and then when it looks like it's spent, gives one last leap. He couldn't believe it.

"Give me another ball."

Apex put a basket of balls down and Dixon very quickly hit four more beautiful shots. Then, while the rest of the executives fought over the club, Apex, Harold and Dixon walked over to the golf shack. Dixon was frowning and shaking his head.

"Well, Dixon?" said Apex.

"That was a disgusting experience, and I'm disgusted with myself for enjoying it."

"What are you talking about?" said Apex. "You were having a ball!"

"Granted," said Dixon. "And I would probably have a ball smoking pot. Those devilish golf clubs are like a drug. They make you think you're something you're not."

"They're fun!" said Apex.

"They're like a basketball that goes through the hoop no matter where you throw it. They're like a baseball bat that always hits home runs. And they can ruin golf."

Harold was concerned.

"How could they ruin golf, Mr. Dixon?"

Dixon counted off the ways on his fingers.

"No more lessons, no more club professionals, no more exhibitions, no more crowds at big tournaments, no more people watching golf on TV, no more competition at any level—because everyone would play the same—and no more incentives for kids to learn the game. I'm sure there are other reasons, but those will do."

"Listen to the man on the soap box," said Apex. "You're breaking my heart. Ribbon's invention'll ruin golf clubs like the bicycle ruined walking. How many sets of these clubs can we sell, Dixon? Twenty-five million? Thirty million?"

Dixon glanced over toward the tee. The executives were fighting like a bunch of kids over whose turn it was.

"Not interested, Apex." Dixon gestured to the executives. "Let's go!"

"Yeah? Well, who needs you guys? We'll make 'em ourselves. Happy bankruptcy!"

Apex and Harold walked to the tee and picked up the set of clubs. They got into Apex's car and joined the traffic jam of expensive cars leaving Milo's Stop 'n Sock.

Harold was still in bed the next morning when Mr. Leroy Dixon called personally. He almost gushed as he invited Harold and Apex to "Come over around 10-ish for a nice chat . . . and bring those marvelous golf clubs with you."

Dixon met them on the front steps of his building. He was bubbling over with friendship and good will.

"So good of you to come!" said Dixon.

He led them across the plush reception room toward a corridor lined with beautifully framed oil paintings of famous athletes and sports personalities. They continued on down the corridor to the conference room. There they met all of the executives who were at Milo's Stop 'n Sock, plus some new ones. They all stood up.

"Gentlemen," said Dixon. "This is Mr. Louis Apex, whom you all know. And this is Mr. Harold Ribbon, whom most of us met yesterday. Now, let's get right down to business. Mr. Ribbon, we are prepared to buy your invention and we are prepared to offer you. . . ."

Harold held up one finger.

"Just a minute, Mr. Dixon, just hold it right there! Why should I sell you my invention? I came to you people in good faith, but I was humiliated and bullied, thrown out, treated as a crackpot. I can't see any good reason to deal with you."

Dixon grinned and decided to play his trump card.

108

"There is a very good reason, Mr. Ribbon—money. We will pay you $100,000 for your invention."

"One hundred thousand dollars!" said Apex. "PEA-NUTS! Listen, Dixon, Ribbon's invention can put all you guys out of business and you know it."

A tall gentlemen with a goatee stood up.

"Let me introduce myself. I am Hugo Axminster, president of the Golfing Association. I think the fact that I'm here tells you how serious we consider this situation to be. For the reasons Dixon outlined yesterday, this invention cannot be marketed."

Harold was upset by the whole situation.

"I thought I was improving golf," said Harold. "I thought I was building a better mousetrap. All I've apparently succeeded in doing is making a lot of people unhappy."

All around the table heads nodded at one another. They agreed with Harold's statement.

Apex leaped to his feet and pounded the table.

"Well, you haven't made me unhappy, Ribbon. Let's just leave these creeps and go make us some golf clubs."

Dixon held up his hand.

"All right, Ribbon, how much?"

Harold's jaw was set. He looked from face to face around the table.

"I'm a very reasonable person. Yesterday you could have had the invention at a reasonable price. But you have made me mad. All right, I'll give you a 'how much'— $1 million for me, and $1 million for Mr. Apex."

The executives cried out in anguish, held their heads in pain and thumped the table. The whole room had exploded into action, except for the imperturbable Dixon.

"Pay it!" he shouted. "Pay it!"

"And one more thing," said Harold over the tumult. "I get to keep the clubs and can use them whenever I feel like it."

The room exploded again. Dixon jumped to his feet.

"That's impossible, Ribbon. Secrecy is everything with an invention like this. We couldn't take the chance."

"Look," said Harold. "The only reason I'm selling the clubs at all is so I can afford to quit my job and play golf. And let's face it, I'm calling the shots. I've got you guys over a barrel."

Dixon looked at Harold malevolently.

"All right!" he barked. "But let's get it in the contract that he can't tell anybody about the clubs. He can't let anyone else use the clubs. And he can't construct any more of the clubs. Agreed, Ribbon?"

"Agreed."

"If any of these terms are violated, we get the money back and all rights to the clubs."

"Agreed. And if you tell anyone about the clubs, I keep the money and I'm free to manufacture."

Dixon's lawyer had been writing furiously on the contract forms, crossing out and writing in. He finally finished them and handed the copies to Dixon who shoved them at Harold.

"Wait a minute!" he bellowed. "What are we getting for our money? A bunch of promises? You're keeping the clubs and we're getting a lot of words."

Harold dumped the contents of a shopping bag onto the table. They were full-scale engineering drawings, schematic photographs, specification sheets, preliminary patent work and three actual mechanisms.

"That's everything but the clubs themselves, and they are in a safe place. All that data is dated and signed."

The men around the table buzzed with excitement as they looked the materials over.

"Okay, Ribbon," Dixon nodded. "Sign the three copies."

Harold and Apex signed the contract and burst out of the front door of the Dixon Company, whooping like Indians.

"Look at that!" said Dixon, as he and the other golf executives watched from the window of the conference room. "The runt and the loudmouth. Well, they haven't heard the end of this."

It was at their victory dinner following the million-dollar contract that Apex brought up the painful subject he'd been worrying about ever since Harold had made his deal with Dixon.

"How are you going to chip and putt?" he asked Harold.

"How am I going to what?" replied Harold.

"Those mechanical marvels of yours are only good for a full swing," said Apex. "How are you going to roll in a side-hiller, get out of a trap or punch one up from the short rough?"

Even golf nuts and fanatics discount the short game. But Apex opened Harold's eyes to the fact that if he was going to compete with the big boys, the super-jocks of golf, his game had to be solid.

Miss Becknell agreed to let Harold have her attic carpeted in Astro Turf. She let him bore into the floorboards and install regulation cups between the joists. Pins with red flags completed the picture.

Then Harold bought a giant blue metal sandbox from a playground supply house and had it placed in the center of the room. It took 84 sacks of white sand to fill the box and each sack was hauled up to the attic by rope.

Putting was no problem. Harold had developed an amazing dexterity in his youth as a pinball machine addict, and this phenomenal touch eventually made him a deadly putter. His unusual pinball background was also responsible for a whole new style of putting. It was a simple but revolutionary technique, the first significant breakthrough since croquet-style putting came on the scene.

Harold simply conceived of, and used, his blade putter as if it were a giant pinball-machine flipper. In the same way as he would urge and caress a gleaming pinball into the super-dooper hole with a flipper, Harold's surgeon fingers would grasp the putter, ground it and then create a fulcrum at the hosel by raising the front part of the blade off the ground. He would then pivot the blade on this fulcrum and simply rotate it back to address position, stroking the ball and sending it forward on the perfect line. Harold's touch was so delicate that the ball would almost die right at the hole and then topple in. Using this technique, he was able to make an unusual number of side-door and back-door cans.

In fact, Harold's pivot-putting method caught on overnight. It took the yips out of golf. Since the club was always grounded, neither the wrists, the arms or the shoulders were involved in the shot. No more jingles, jangles, heebie-jeebies or gulping-sobbing muscle spasms. No more standing over the ball for 17 minutes. With pivot putting, the proper line was locked in and the shot became mechanical.

Harold had a much more serious problem with sand, because there was no application from pinballs or any other experience in his life. Simply taking a wedge and attempting a sand shot was no more possible than before, purely on the basis of his zero coordination and lack of strength. Pivot blasting didn't work either because there was no real power in that technique, certainly not enough to lift a ball out of sand. And it was illegal to ground a club in a sand trap.

And so Miss Becknell's attic became a battlefield once again. Harold blasted balls off the walls and the ceiling. He knocked out windows and smashed lamps. He would set the programmed sand wedge into motion with all of its astonishing power and fly balls out of the sandbox so hard they would richochet off the walls, like bullets in a western movie.

Little by little, Harold learned to hit behind the ball. On a touchy little three-foot pop shot that called for a one-third swing, Harold would give it the full arc. Attacking the ball with his usual ferocity, he would hit as much as two feet behind the ball, sending up a wall of sand that drenched the entire green. But the ball would loop like a piece of fluff and land dead at, or in, the hole.

Apex dropped by occasionally to check Harold's progress. One afternoon he watched Harold drop 17 straight pivot putts ranging from five to 35 feet. From a safe distance he saw a dozen blasts of different lengths either stony or in. He drove out to Milo's with Harold and witnessed an amazing exhibition of power and accuracy. Harold could now hit shots from 50 feet to over 400 yards in a dead straight line. He was stunned by the caliber of golf he had just seen.

"Harold, baby," he said. "I know you've never been on an actual golf course, but you're ready. You are ready for anybody. There's a little amateur tournament down in the next county starting day after tomorrow. Some pretty good shooters down there. Go get your feet wet."

Harold parked his bicycle in front of the Cockle County Country Club and walked inside. He was wearing brown gabardine knickers, a matching hat, and red and white checked stockings. His multi-colored clubs were in a thin, white cloth "Sunday bag."

Just inside the front door was a card table with a sign reading "Registration." A severe looking young matron was sitting behind the table, very busy with paperwork. She finally looked up at Harold, grimaced, and said impatiently, "I'm sorry, but the course is closed for a tournament. Come back next Wednesday."

"But I'm here to play in the tournament," said Harold. She looked him up and down with distaste.

"Look," she said. "This is an important golf tournament, the Cockle County Open. Every hot-shot golfer in the country is here: Leroy Frotz, Herman Snaddler, Marve Bleetely—all big gunners. Why don't you just run along to some costume party?"

Harold held out a $10 bill.

"I have my registration fee."

She sighed and grabbed the money from his hand.

"Name?"

"Harold Ribbon."

"Where do you play golf?"

"Milo's Stop 'n Sock."

"Milo's Stop 'n Sock? Oh, swell!"

She wrote down the information. Then she looked at the large chart on the wall behind her.

"Okay. Harold Ribbon from Milo's Stop 'n Sock. There's been a cancellation and I can tee you off right now. You'll play in a foursome with Marve Bleetely, the defending champion, and don't say I didn't warn you. You play 18 holes today and 18 tomorrow. If you make the cut, you go 36 on Sunday."

Marve Bleetely and the other two members of Harold's foursome were already on the first tee. Marve was the champ, a fat cat, as big as a house. He was dressed from head to toe in yellow—hat, sweater, slacks and shoes—and he was juggling a few balls for the crowd as Harold walked up onto the tee. Bleetely stopped juggling, looked at Harold, looked back at the crowd, then threw up his arms.

"I give up!"

The crowd laughed. Bleetely bared his teeth in a gigantic grin as the loudspeaker announced the foursome.

"On the tee, Marvin Bleetely, defending Cockle County Open Champion, playing out of Cockle County Country Club."

Bleetely stuck out his tongue, grinned and held both hands up and wiggled the fingers. The loudspeaker announcement continued.

"Ed Orson of the Rondalay Links, Bart Schwartz of Blue Acres Country Club, and Harold Ribbon from Milo's Stop 'n Sock."

The crowd roared with laughter. Then Bleetely teed up and socked one down the center. The crowd applauded. Orson and Schwartz followed with average drives. Now Harold teed up and promptly blasted one that went by Bleetely's ball on the fly. Bleetely turned to the awe-struck crowd and shrugged.

"Drive for show, putt for dough."

On the first hole Bleetely laid his approach shot six feet from the pin. Harold hit a skyball stiff. Bleetely missed his putt. Harold tapped it in backhanded.

The second hole was a long par-5 of some 550 yards with big trees, water and sand trouble for the first 300. Harold simply drove over all of it. When the other three players finally got up to where his ball had landed, Harold calmly took out a 5-iron and hit a towering shot that landed dead in the hole for a double eagle. Bleetely got a bogey 6 to lose four strokes in one swoop.

The par-3 third hole was 215 yards long. Harold got a hole-in-one, which gave him a seven-stroke lead over Bleetely after only three holes.

On the fourth hole Bleetely lost his gallery. Harold had hit a long blast straight down the center, and Bleetely had yelled "Lucky!" The crowd was stunned and showed its anger by growling at him. After that, Bleetely's game began to fall apart. He sliced his next drive, found sand with his third shot, and ended up with a double bogey.

As the afternoon wore on, Bleetely grew more and more disheveled. The ominous growl of the gallery kept him from slurring Harold's game, but it did not keep him from throwing and breaking clubs. His breath began to come in rasps and his face was beet red with rage and frustration.

Meanwhile, Harold continued to boom out one glorious shot after another. His drives were dead straight and way out. His approach shots were gigantic skyballs, as high as they were long, and his pivot putts were either in or hanging. Harold's picture book swing also drew a lot of gallery comment.

"Looks like Ace Perkins out there."

"He copied Perkins. Or maybe Perkins copied him."

Finally, they reached the 18th green. Bleetely had by now degenerated into a pathetic, rumpled fat man with his shirttail out. Harold rifled in about a 25-foot putt and the crowd cheered. Bleetely missed his four-footer and shrugged. He was a broken man. The loudspeaker called out the scores.

"Bleetely—84; Orson—78; Schwartz—74; Ribbon—a new course record, 63."

The crowd cheered. It had a new hero. As Harold was leaving the green surrounded by his fans, the matron from the registration desk confronted him.

"I say it was luck," she said.

Harold shook his head.

"Lady," he said. "There was no luck to it. I'll show you tomorrow."

On the 18th green the following day, Harold lined up a

putt of maybe 30 feet. He pivoted the putter and it was good all the way. The loudspeaker announced the scores again.

"Bleetely—76; Orson—78; Schwartz—73; Ribbon—62, a new course record, breaking the record he set just yesterday."

Again the crowd went crazy over the new star. The lady from the registration desk pushed through the crowd and grabbed Harold's arm possessively.

"It wasn't luck, was it, Harold?"

"Ma'am, I told you it wasn't."

Later, in the locker room, a call came in for Harold. It was Dixon.

"Harold, what in the world do you think you're doing? I just got the report on the radio about your 125 for 36 holes."

"It's true, Mr. Dixon. I'm playing beautiful golf."

"You can't play competitive golf with those fraudulent clubs! You're going to get a beautiful lump on your head if you play any more!"

"You shouldn't talk that way, Mr. Dixon. There's no reason I can't play in competition."

"Listen, Harold, don't you understand? You're not a golfer, you're a cheater, a faker, a fraud!"

"Mr. Dixon, I figured out how to make those clubs do all those things, and there's nothing fake about it. You should have been here."

"Well, don't worry your weird head, I'll be there."

Leroy Dixon's feelings about Harold Ribbon were as rabid as they were negative. The two men were total opposites, poles apart. Leroy was a big, broad-shouldered jock, an ex-footballer; Harold was built like Rumplestiltskin. Leroy had classic, chiseled features; Harold's were more like Van Gogh's "Potato Eaters." Leroy was a fraternity man and a conservative; Harold was an independent and a liberal. Leroy had a London tailor; Harold dressed like a clown. And so it went.

But the unforgiveable sin—the one factor that gave

116

Leroy strong motivation for considering the death of Harold Ribbon by lingering and painful means—was Harold's desecration of the shrine, the altar: golf.

The fact that this peasant, this water boy had just fired the best 36-hole score in the history of amateur golf by flagrant fraud was nothing less than sacrilege. It must be dealt with.

In the meantime, word of Harold's two great rounds had drawn a sizable gallery for the final round. The first tee was surrounded. Dixon was standing in the first row as Harold came through the crowd.

"On the tee, Mr. Harold Ribbon!" boomed the loudspeaker.

Harold teed up and waggled the club expertly. He swung, missed the ball, swung back like a left-hander and connected, hitting a line drive backwards over the crowd and smashing a picture window on the second story of the clubhouse. Dixon guffawed. The rest of the crowd was stunned and silent. Bleetely seized the opportunity.

"No, no, Harold, that way!" he said, pointing toward the first green.

The crowd laughed.

Harold teed up again and this time he hit an awful little grounder, but at least in the right direction.

His game had completely disintegrated. He dubbed, he skied, he hooked, he sliced. His beautiful Ace Perkins swing was gone. He found every trap. He plunked balls into the water hazards. He sent balls bounding over fences. Dixon, who stood in the front row for every shot, led the laughter and ridicule.

Apex pushed through the crowd and walked along with Harold.

"Are the clubs busted, Harold?" he asked.

"No. I know what's happening. Thank heavens this is the last hole. I'll meet you back at the motel in 15 minutes."

Harold dubbed his way to the green and somehow got the ball into the hole. As he walked off the green, the loudspeaker blared the scores.

"Bleetely—73; Orson—71; Schwartz—75; and yesterday's leader, Harold Ribbon—100!"

"One hundred blows!" said Dixon. "What are you going to try for this afternoon?'"

"Mr. Dixon," said Harold, "why don't you stop interfering with my golf game?"

"In the first place, Ribbon, it's not your golf game, it's those phony clubs. And I wouldn't miss your afternoon round for that million dollars you swindled me out of," said Dixon, grinning and holding up his briefcase.

Back in his motel room, Harold explained the situation to Apex.

"Here's the story: You noticed that briefcase Dixon carried around with him? He's got some kind of powerful magnet in it, probably an electromagnet."

"What did it do?" asked Alex.

"It kept the gyroscopes from functioning. It just plain neutralized them."

"Well, what are you going to do?" said Alex.

"When I get home, I'll make new mechanisms out of plastic," said Harold, "but for now I'll have to insulate. I'll need some nail polish. Get me about 10 bottles."

Apex took off for the nearest drug store. Then Harold pulled out his wallet, opened it and produced a miniature tool kit. He quickly unscrewed the faceplates on his clubs and carefully lifted out all of the mechanisms. As soon as Apex returned with the nail polish, the two men began feverishly painting.

The crowd for the afternoon finale was larger and more raucous than it had been in the morning. The news of Harold's horrible downfall had drawn the vultures. Dixon was in position in the front row, his briefcase in hand. Bleetely and the other two members of the foursome drove. Harold stepped to the tee. Instead of the classic silence of this situation, the air was filled with snickering and ridicule.

"Bet you can't hit the clubhouse again!"

"Run for your lives!"

Harold was unperturbed. He addressed the ball, went

118

into that beautiful swing and connected. It started low and began to rise. The hole was 370 yards long. The ball bounced in front of the green, rolled up toward the pin and stopped about a foot away. For a long moment there was a silence. The crowd didn't know how to react. Then came a great animal roar of approval. Dixon was stunned. He shook the briefcase, then put it down and stomped on it.

Harold's game was again perfection. His approach shots were on the stick all the way; they even grabbed as they hit. His only two chip shots for the round both hung on the lip. His one sand shot went into the hole. He took 22 putts. On the 18th green he lined up his longest putt of the day, a 15-footer. He pivot-tapped and it went in the center of the cup. He picked the ball out of the hole, put it in his mouth and walked over to Leroy Dixon. Harold puffed his cheeks out and then expelled the ball. It bounced off Dixon's chest. The crowd went wild. The loudspeaker blared the scores.

". . . and for Ribbon, 60, a new course record, and a 72-hole total of 285 for the Cockle County Open Championship."

The Cockle County Open Championship launched the most amazing golfing career of all time. Harold quickly swept the state title and a month later won the National Amateur by 20 strokes. He capped his first year of competitive golf by winning eight straight professional tournaments, the Masters and the National Open. He became the first amateur since Johnny Goodman to win the Open.

Harold's harassment at the hands of Dixon and the Establishment naturally increased. The physical attacks were easy to handle. Harold turned Miss Becknell's boarding house and grounds into one big electronic booby trap. There were warning devices, closed-circuit television with monitors in every room, electric shock devices, water-squirting devices and hidden pressure guns that could expel golf balls at bone-cracking speed.

There was tacit agreement in both camps that the police

would never be brought in. The Establishment feared a security leak concerning the clubs. Harold feared a voiding of the contract. Harold also feared that the clubs would be stolen, and if they were he could not make new ones. This was a definite specification of the contract. So between tournaments the clubs were kept in a big safe which sat in the center of Miss Becknell's living room. The safe had been purchased shortly after the Masters victory when one of Dixon's goons had penetrated as far as the front door before being cold-cocked by a fusillade of Maxflis. He had surmounted the electronic obstacles by insulating himself in a plastic suit. The golf ball gun that got him was activated by a mechanical trip. A roof-mounted gun of the same type crippled an enemy helicopter that was hovering above the rooming house while attempting to land three hoodlums on the roof. The copter crashed in a swamp outside of town. There was one other major penetration—a tunnel. Harold determined exactly where in the basement the breakthrough would occur. When it did, a garden hose was stuck into the hole and turned on full blast. The professional safecracker in the tunnel barely escaped with his life.

Harold got used to the physical harassment but worried continually over Dixon's allegation that he was a cheater. Harold reasoned that his success was due simply to the fact that his equipment was superior. Did not the fastest car or boat or plane generally win the race? And what about other improvements made in sports equipment that resulted in better performance? Hadn't the plastic pole pushed the pole vault record up two feet? The vaulters who first used these poles were not called cheaters. In baseball, deep-welled mitts had become commonplace. Players using these mitts certainly had an advantage over the early-day players who fielded bare-handed, but nobody accused them of cheating.

Harold was concerned that golf clubs like his were not available to the public, but he dismissed this thought on the grounds that business was business. Dixon also liked to point out that Harold's clubs violated section 2, 2b, of the USGA official rules. This section states that "movable parts are prohibited, that no part of the club may be movable, separable or capable of adjustment during a round of play." Harold argued that this had to do with degree of loft and had nothing to do with his clubs. His clubs were not, in that sense, adjustable. But the harassment and the recriminations continued.

Still, Harold continued to pile up victories and shatter every record in the book. He was in his apartment one day, gazing moodily out the window, when Apex dropped by to see him.

"Oh, hello, Louis. Have you heard the news? The head of the USGA called and told me that I was a pro because Milo put up a sign that says, 'Milo's Stop 'n Sock —Home of Harold Ribbon.' "

"So what?"

"So what! So I can't enter any more amateur tournaments. I can't play on the Walker Cup team. I can't make any more Grand Slams. That's so what! And Leroy Dixon just called to congratulate me on becoming a *professional* cheater!"

Harold sat down on his bed in despair. Apex pulled up a chair, facing him.

"Listen, Harold, you're too good to be an amateur. Leave the amateur tournaments to the amateurs. Believe me, Harold, if any of those amateurs were good enough, they'd turn pro, like that!" Apex snapped his fingers for emphasis.

"And now that you are a pro, Harold, let me be the first to make you a little business proposition. I want to manufacture Harold Ribbon golf clubs, golf balls and knickers."

Harold looked at Apex as if he were out of his mind.

"Harold Ribbon golf clubs! Louis, you know perfectly well the terms of my contract with Dixon and the boys. I can't ever make any more of these clubs."

"I don't mean clubs like that," said Louis. "I mean regular golf clubs."

"You mean, I use clubs run by transistors and gyroscopes and you sell clubs *without* them?" said Harold.

"Exactly!"

Harold stared at Apex.

"I'm going to have to ask you to leave, Mr. Apex."

"Hold it!" said Apex. "Sit down, Harold! Look, Ace Perkins and dozens of other golfers have got clubs on the market with their names on them. Right?"

"Right," said Harold.

"Okay, so when Ace is hot, everybody runs out and buys Ace's clubs. Does swinging with their hero's clubs make a difference in their golf games? Emphatically yes! But for only one reason: confidence! The guy is swinging in a positive frame of mind. He expects better performance with his new clubs and he gets it!"

"Well, I don't know," said Harold.

"I'll bring some design sketches over tomorrow. Thousands of golfers are already painting their clubs wild colors to look like yours. Let's make 'em available in baked enamel. And colors are darn practical. How could anyone confuse a 6-iron with a 9-iron if one is orange and one is blue?"

"Okay," said Harold. He grinned at Apex. He felt a lot better.

The Apex Sporting Goods Company doubled, tripled, quadrupled and was finally about 20 times its original size, employing more than 300 people. Harold Ribbon clubs and equipment were selling at a record pace all over the world.

In Harold's third year of big time golf he won title after title. He continued to win every tournament he entered. He swept both the Masters and the Open for the third straight year, and he won his third British Open.

It was in this, his third big year, that "Harold's Horde" became something of a problem. Five thousand people packed solidly around one green made the field movement of players, caddies, officials, reporters and television and radio personnel quite difficult. "Harold's Horde" magnified the problem to incredible proportions, because it consisted of defectors from all of the other groups. The only people left watching the other pros were caddies, wives and sweethearts—and often even they would go over the hill. When Harold was on the tee more than 25,000 fans would be in attendance, enough to fill some football stadiums. And they loved Harold with a fiercer love than that shown any other sports figure in history. Because Harold never let them down.

A retired army general, familiar with the mass movement of troops, came up with a partial solution to the "Harold's Horde" problem. When a fan purchased a tournament ticket, the ticket was either red, white or blue. The color designated the holes on which the fan was allowed: red on 1, 4, 7, 10, 13 and 16; white on 2, 5, 8, 11, 14 and 17; and blue on 3, 6, 9, 12, 15 and 18. Thus, after a given hole, there was not the frenzied mass movement of 25,000 people hysterically fighting for position. Instead, only a third of that number moved at one time, making it somewhat easier for club and tournament officials to cope with the situation.

Harold's third year on the tour had two big purposes as far as he was concerned. He discussed them the day before the National Open in a television interview with the famed golf commentator, Harrison Romaine.

"Well, Harold," said Romaine, "your amazing career is steaming along at full speed. Do you have any special plans this year?"

"Yes, Harrison, are you familiar with the words 'the impregnable quadrilateral of golf?' "

"I don't believe so, Harold."

"Those are words concocted to describe Bobby Jones' performance in 1930 when he won the British and American Amateurs and Opens. It was said that Jones had 'stormed the impregnable quadrilateral of golf.' "

"Well, what's your point, Harold."

"I am going to storm what I call 'the impossible one and a half.' One hundred and fifty straight tournament victories."

Romaine shook his head in wonderment.

"Well, Harold, you certainly are the greatest golfer in the world. And think of all the money you've won!"

"Mr. Romaine, I haven't won a red cent! I don't accept any prize money. I'm fabulously wealthy, so I don't see any point in dragging home a few paltry extra thousands. I just ask the tournament committees to split it up among the also-rans. You know—Ace Perkins and the rest. Those guys really need the money. I don't."

"One more thing, Harold. You'll tee off in the National Open tomorrow morning. That's the big one, the one that means the most. Don't you consider the Open something extra special?"

"No, Mr. Romaine, it's just another tournament—except that this will be the fourth year in a row that I'll have won it, which nobody has ever done before."

"You're sure you're going to win, aren't you, Harold?"

"Bet on it! Get out the family jewels! As a matter of fact, I'm going to try to be so far ahead after 36 holes that it will turn the whole thing into a farce."

In the boardroom at Dixon Sporting Goods, Dixon and several others were watching the television interview. Dixon was pacing up and down muttering to himself. The room was in complete disarray. Dixon and his men had been there for hours discussing the Harold Ribbon problem. Empty coffee cups and overflowing ashtrays littered the table along with the remains of meals that had been sent in. The men were in their shirt sleeves with ties askew. Dixon stood up and faced the other men.

"That arrogant swine has made a mockery out of a great noble sport. Our National Open is the most important golf tournament in the world. It is the ambition of every golfer to win the Open. It assures him of his place in golfing history. And now we're faced with the prospect of Harold Ribbon winning it four times in a row—something no man has been able to do. He must be stopped.

"We have got to disgrace Ribbon publicly," Dixon remonstrated. "We have got to show the world that he is a cheat, a fraud and a phony. Gentlemen, simply snatching the clubs by one means or another does not suit our purpose any more. We have got to pull off the old switcheroo."

With that, Dixon produced a set of clubs. They looked like Harold's. Each one was a different wild, bright color. The bag was exactly like the cheap Sunday bag Harold had used ever since winning the Cockle County Open.

"Now," said Dixon, "these clubs are identical to Ribbon's. We've taken hundreds of photographs of Ribbon's clubs with hidden cameras and telescopic lenses, and these are identical down to the most minute dents and scratches."

"What about golf balls?" someone asked Dixon.

He unzipped the ball compartment and took out a couple of balls. "Harold Ribbon autographed balls. They're the only kind he uses."

"Okay," Dixon continued. "The clubs, the bag and the balls are identical to the ones Ribbon uses. If we can pull off the old switcheroo, Ribbon will tee off in front of all those people and make a fool out of himself. It will be the end of the foul career of the great Harold Ribbon."

The morning of the first round of the Open at Portmanteau Country Club was a madhouse scene. The tennis courts had been converted into a giant refreshment center. Beer and soft drink trucks were disgorging their cargoes. Grandstands had been erected near the 18th green and workmen were putting in the final touches with much clattering and banging. Out on the lawn beyond the terrace a huge candy-striped tent had been erected.

It was perfect golf weather. The massive oak trees lining the fairways seemed to be in super focus against the brilliant blue of the sky. The course itself had been lengthened and toughened, and it was in superb condition. The deep emerald of the fairways and greens was punctuated by 125 gleaming white mica-sand traps—17 of which had been newly created for the event. They all had deep furrows and five-inch lips. Portmanteau Creek meandered through 14 of the 18 holes. It was not only wide and deep, but rushing. At various points out on the course orange maintenance trucks and equipment were busy. Greens were being dewed-off with bamboo poles. Difficult pin positions were being set. Everything was being double-checked. The air was filled with the smell of freshly mown grass.

Behind the grandstand near the first tee was an orange pickup truck. Next to the ball-washer was a large sprinkler. Harold Ribbon's caddie leaned his bag against the grandstand, unzipped the golf-ball compartment and removed a half-dozen balls. He walked over to the washer, put two balls in and began churning them.

Suddenly the sprinkler went on full blast, engulfing the caddie in a sheet of water. At that moment two men, both dressed in Portmanteau Country Club maintenance overalls, leaped out of the orange pickup truck and ran over to where Harold's clubs were leaning against the grandstand. One man grabbed Harold's clubs and ducked out of sight behind some bushes. The other, with a bag of fake clubs, took off across the course as fast as he could lumber. Harold's caddie spotted him and took chase. He nabbed the culprit with a flying tackle, hit him three times and then flipped him into Portmanteau Creek.

Harold's tee time was listed on the program as 10:15 A.M. At 8:30 his fans were in full force, awaiting his arrival by jet helicopter. By 9:00 more than 10,000 of the faithful surrounded the first tee, the first fairway and the first green 445 yards away. By 10:00 the number of fans had doubled. In the front ranks of the crowd at the tee were Dixon and several other members of The Establishment. Dixon and the others were delighted about something. They were grinning and laughing like one big happy family.

The public address system came on.

"On the tee Mr. Bull Babson, Mr. Ace Perkins and Mr. Harold Ribbon."

The crowd cheered wildly, but Harold was nowhere to be seen.

"I wonder where Harold is?" said Babson.

"Man, I'd be just as happy if he didn't show," said Perkins.

A roar went up from the clubhouse, and Harold was borne toward the tee on the shoulders of his fans. Most of

them were wearing knickers. They were all chanting wildly, "Rib-bon! Rib-bon! Rib-bon! Rib-bon!"

"Wow!" said Babson. "Look at Harold's Horde!"

"Well, he deserves it," said Perkins wistfully. "He's
the best."

Harold was deposited at the tee. He was magnificent in
dayglow purple—hat, shirt, knickers, stockings and shoes.
His hat was pulled way down over his eyes. He shook
hands with Perkins.

"Ace-kid!"

He shook hands with Babson.

"Bull-baby!"

He grinned at Perkins and Babson and said, "Well, to
paraphrase the great Walter Hagen: which one of you cats
is going to come in second?"

Harold, Perkins, Babson and the crowd roared over
this. The starter intoned:

"Mr. Bull Babson."

Babson teed up, addressed the ball and boomed one
down the center.

"Mr. Ace Perkins."

Perkins smacked one down the center.

"Mr. Harold Ribbon."

The announcement was greeted by a roar of applause
and shouting. The Dixon group could hardly stand it—
they were so delighted at what was about to happen to
Harold. Harold teed the ball up very deliberately. He set
himself in position and addressed the ball. Then he spotted
Dixon and the group.

"Well, Mr. Dixon. I didn't know you were one of my
fans."

"I can hardly wait to see you hit that ball, Ribbon."

"Okay," said Harold. He addressed the ball, then
stopped and held the club out like it was a fishing rod. He
waggled it back and forth. He squinted at it. He shrugged.
He addressed the ball again. The crowd was silent. He
started his picture book swing, smacked the ball and completed a classic and perfect follow-through. It was a big
hit, a long, soaring shot straight down the center and well

127

past the shots of Babson and Perkins. The crowd said, "Ahhhhhh!" and burst into a roar of applause. Harold put his arms around Perkins and Babson and the three started walking down the fairway. Everyone seemed to be grinning and enjoying the scene.

By themselves on the first tee were Dixon and The Establishment members. Dixon was stunned. He froze, with one hand on his forehead and his mouth wide open.

The others were shrugging and discussing the situation in disbelief.

Dixon signaled with his hand. "Bring me the clubs!"

A henchman brought him Harold's clubs and a screwdriver. Dixon briskly unscrewed the faceplate of the driver and laid bare the works.

"See?" said one of Dixon's men. "See all the gyroscopes and transistors? There's no mistake. These are definitely Ribbon's clubs, boss!"

"I know! I know!" said Dixon tragically.

He turned to the group. "Do you men know what's happened? Do you realize what's happened?"

The men were baffled. They shook their heads in unison.

"Ribbon has been playing with those phony clubs for more than three years now, and they've actually taught him how to play! He really is the greatest golfer in the world!"

In the distance they could barely see the tiny figure as it swung the club. Then the vast gallery roared its approval and surged on.